© Copyright 2003 Johnny Lac. All rights reserved.

No part of this publication may be reproduced, stored in a retrieval system, or transmitted, in any form or by any means, electronic, mechanical, photocopying, recording, or otherwise, without the written prior permission of the author.

Printed in Victoria, Canada

```
National Library of Canada Cataloguing in Publication

Lac, Johnny, 1954- Under the Vietnam flags / Johnny Flags.

ISBN 1-55395-521-8

1. Lac, Johnny, 1954-   2. Vietnamese Conflict, 1961-1975—
Personal narratives,
Vietnamese.   3. Vietnam—History—1975-   I. Title.

DS559.914.L32A3 2003     959.704'3'092    C2003-900104-0
```

TRAFFORD

This book was published *on-demand* in cooperation with Trafford Publishing. On-demand publishing is a unique process and service of making a book available for retail sale to the public taking advantage of on-demand manufacturing and Internet marketing. **On-demand publishing** includes promotions, retail sales, manufacturing, order fulfilment, accounting and collecting royalties on behalf of the author.

Suite 6E, 2333 Government St., Victoria, B.C. V8T 4P4, CANADA
Phone   250-383-6864   Toll-free   1-888-232-4444 (Canada & US)
Fax   250-383-6804   E-mail   sales@trafford.com
Web site   www.trafford.com   TRAFFORD PUBLISHING IS A DIVISION OF TRAFFORD
HOLDINGS LTD.
Trafford Catalogue #03-1236   www.trafford.com/robots/03-1236.html

10   9   8   7   6   5   4

Special Edition and Bestseller

JOHNNY LAC

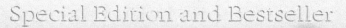

For what has been through,
Thick and thin,
Facts remain as solid as mountains and rivers,
Unlike clouds in the air.

UNDER THE VIETNAM FLAGS

Also, with thanks together and that I, too, am a part of the circle:

Front cover poem translated:
Dr. Patrick Cham
Desktop publishing, photographs scanning and graphics work:
Jammes Wong
Front, back covers and spine graphic design:
Leo De-Min Xue
Front, back covers and spine original arts design:
Johnny Lac
Photographs copied from:
The Phuoc-Duc School Alumni Association in Toronto & Los Angeles
Vietnamese tourist handbook # 184 VHTT 24/04/2000
Thai-Khac Chuong (Former UPI photographer)
Vietnamese newspaper #174 RA 27/04/2000
V N A / courtesy John Spragens, Jr
Mae Seto Quan (Canada)
Thuong-Lam Ly (Vietnam)
Khanh-Phat Ta (France)
Wendy Luc (Canada)
Wendy Lei (Canada)
Johnny Lac (Canada)

ஐ⊙ஜ

Published by
Trafford on-demand publishing service

Printed in Canada

Especially For _____

With Warm Wishes From

_____

Date _____

This book is dedicated to:

My surrogate uncle **Nhan, Kim-Tan**, and aunt **Luu, Thi-Hoa**, who saved my life during the *Vietnam War*, and my brother-in-law **Ly, Hien-Nap**, and my sister **Ta-Kim**, who were ongoing supporting me and saving me from the war, and my parents **Ta, Thanh-Ha** and **Lac-Thuat** for their care. Also, to thank my nephew **Ly, Tuyen-Binh**, who shared everything in the same boat in this journey with me from escaping Vietnam to the land.

A special thanks to **The United Nations High Commissioner**, **The International Red Cross**, and **The Catholic Mission Team** *for refugees*, and *the news media that helped to tell the world about the victims of the war. I would also like to thank the humanity of the Canadian people!*

When fighting begins from a small group, sometimes
it ends in a bigger fight. Like the world we are living in now.
Peace, no war. Please no war.

Quand on commence à lutter dans un petit groupe, quelque fois
ca finit par s'agrandir. Tout comme le monde oú nous habitons
maintenant. La paix, pas de guerre. S'il vous plaît pas de guerre.

Johnny Lac. 2002. Vancouver, B.C. Canada.

[Translated by Lorraine Seddon / Susie C. Car]

每當小紛爭開始引發而未能平息的時候，

最終的禍害會導致無法挽回的局面。

但人類需要置身在一個美好的世界里。

願和平，無戰亂。

壬午年　加拿大　駱鐘福留題

CONTENTS

The Song of the Life Where We Are	I, II, III
Poem translated from English to Chinese (The Song of the Life Where We Are)	IV
A Word From The Author	V, VI, VII
My Life in Saigon and Cholon	VIII, IX, X, XI, XII, XIII
S-shaped Vietnam map	XIV
Introduction	1-2
Climate in South and North Vietnam	2-3
Major Products in Vietnam	3
Vietnamese History	4-7
Vietnamese Language, Cultural, Education and Religions	7-9
Vietnam Life in Saigon and Cholon--HoChiMinh City	9-19
A Favorite Part of Vung-Tau Beach	20-22
The Vietnam War in 1968	23-24
My School Damaged in 1968	25-26
End of the War in Sight	27-28
My Life in Tuy-Hoa--Phu-Yen	29-32
My Return to Saigon	33-36
Vietnam War North and South	37-38
Map of key battles of the Vietnam War 1957 to 1975	39
Cargo Suppliers during The Vietnam War	40-42

The Vietnam War in 1975	43-44
The Fall of Saigon	44-45
War Ends April 30, 1975	45-50
The Continuing Conflict Trouble on Their Way	47
Citizens Forced by Communists	51-52
Money Available Under Communists	52-53
Life Under Communism Compared to "Capitalism"	53-54
The Black Market	54
Small Shops Appearing	55-56
My Surrogate Uncle Nhan and Family Closed Their Store Under Communist's Force	56-58
My Brother-in-law Forced Out of Business by Communists	58-60
My Uncle Forced to Change His Life	60-66
Literature, Art and Music Under Communist's Controls	67-68
People Planning to Escape	69-71
Our First Plan to Escape from Cholon	72-73
Our Second Plan to Escape From Cantho	74
A Tragic Escape	75-76
Bribing the Government	77
Our Third Plan to Escape From Cantho	78-79
Preparing to Leave Cantho	79-82
Our Departure	82
Map of our Sailing Tracks	83
Life on the Seas--from May 30 to June 13, 1979	84-103
Reaching Land on Keramut	104-105

Kuku Island Refugee Camp	106-107
Life on Kuku Island	107-115
Applying for a New Country of Residence	115-116
Pulau Galang Island Refugee Camp	117-119
Pulau Galang to Singapore	120-121
Singapore to Canada	122-123
My First Day in Edmonton, Canada	123-124
Arrival in Vancouver	124-125
Life in Vancouver	125-136
Vietnam Today and in the Future	137-145
Thanks to All	146-147
Peace	148
Poem translated from English to Chinese (Peace)	149
The Gift	150
Poem translated from English to Chinese (The Gift)	151
Children	152-153
Poem translated from English to Chinese (Children)	154
Our Past	155
Poem translated from English to Chinese (Our Past)	156
Synopsis	157-158

I

The Song Of The Life Where We Are

*(Written to all of Vietnamese refugees,
and all people suffering in wars)*

Light the torch into life
It symbolizes the origin of our being!
Life created me;
I created life.

Look that sea
A mountainous wave which rises and falls;
It imparts an omen what a life is to be.

Heed that water
A raging wave which shouts and roars;
It appears like a tune of what your life would be.

Let's sing high a song
The life where we are,
Reformed mission sparks light the life;
Be immortal to sing the song of the life where we are.

II

Recall in the past:
A signal fire used to make me grown,
In the flames of war,
Blood, flesh and tears;
Leave country for town;
Living in a transitional period,
Hard, perilous and mournful.
A thoroughfare of life as it were a poem
The sound of the song,
The life where we are,
...Forever

Despite
Caused to flee from war,
And fly for refuge,
... Present

Caused to run after war,
And seek for struggle,
...Future

III

Pleasure to live with thou,
Sings on, the life where we are.
Let's___
Light the torch into life;
Let's sing the praises of life!
Life created me;
I created life.

By
Johnny Lac
Vancouver, British Columbia.
Canada
December 1999.

~~

IV

生命之歌

駱鍾福

寫給每一位的越南難民和所有遭受戰爭國家的人民

燃點生命火炬 —— 這是象徵生命的起源吧!
生命創造我,
我創造生命
看,那浪濤起伏的浩海,像它告知你生命裡的預兆
聽,那驚鳴呼喚的海嘯,像它啟示你生命裡的樂章
齊奏起一首生命之歌,
讓自己改革使命;把生命燃起火花,
唱一首不停而永恆不滅的生命之歌。

憶往昔:
生長在烽火烈戰的我,
是血是肉還是淚;
離鄉別井,過渡時期,
是辛是險還是悲。
人生道路上就像一首寫不完的生命之歌。

儘管 ——
為了逃亡而投奔怒海,
為了追求理想而奮鬥;
這都是為了奔向萬里,
奔向前程。
投入一箇我最喜愛的國度裡,
高歌歡唱一首愛的生命之歌,
大家齊來燃點生命火炬!
讓生命創造我,
我創造生命。

(稿於溫哥華市,十二月一九九九年)

A WORD FROM THE AUTHOR

The word **Vietnam** is well known since it had a long war. Just think of the fall of Saigon on April 30, 1975, it is unforgettable because it was tragic. Everyday, people see movies, watch television shows and read books about **Vietnam** as the stories are endlessly fascinating.

This is a true story of my near death experience while escaping from Vietnam. I searched in the library for books about Vietnamese history, so that is where some of my knowledge comes from. The story of my journey and eventual settlement in Canada began in the spring of 1980. I am a worker in Environmental Services Department. During my shift with a group of pear workers in a peer tutoring program at British Columbia's Children's Hospital in Vancouver, British Columbia, Canada. My tutor would routinely ask me to talk about my experiences, to help me improve my English.

VI

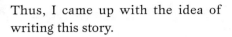

Thus, I came up with the idea of writing this story.

Forced to remember events I had long since suppressed, it was then I decided to unpack the notes I had taken. I kept a daily record of my thoughts and experiences from the time I began my escape from Cholon on May 27, 1979. A simple learning tool at first, the journals became the foundation for a more lengthy explanation of my long struggle to escape post-war South Vietnam.

I am especially grateful to my friends Max Lomas and Don Payzant volunteer tutors and friends from the Hospital, for their helpful suggestions and proofreading skills.

It gives me a great deal of pride to write my first book in English about my life. This book also includes three poems written by my children. The poems "**Peace**" and "**the Gift**" written by my son Jay, when he was nine, and "**Children**" written by my daughter Kay, when she was eight, are written to all parents, children and people of the world. All three poems were originally published in 2000, in The Voice of Overseas Chinese, in Taiwan. My own poems — "The song of the Life

Where We Are", and "Our Past" dedicated to all the Vietnamese refugees and fighting people in the world are included in this book, after first appearing in The Voice..., in December of 1999. The photographs and illustrations help the reader understand the natural beauty of Vietnam, and my sadness when I was forced to leave it all behind.

Growing up in a peaceful country like Canada is easy to take peace, good health and happiness for granted. Yet, millions suffer through war, illness and famine around the world. My thoughts and prayers are with everyone for whom peace is elusive, and for the hope that it will become more bountiful in the future.

Thank you finally to all those who have supported me since my journey began. *I wish you peace and joy.*

Sincerely,

Johnny Lac
May 2003, Vancouver, B.C. Canada.

VIII

My Life in Saigon and Cholon

I love Saigon and Cholon, and I will not forget all the stories *from my childhood*. Also, I remember many people I knew there during our longest war, for Saigon was my hometown where I was born in 1954 and where I spent all my life until 1979.

I grew up in a loving family with my parents. A good circumstance never lasted long, my father just passed away in Mount Saint Joseph Hospital in Vancouver, British Columbia on August 01, 2002 at the age of eighty-six. There are five generations in our home; he left his wife, three sons and three daughters and more than forty grandchildren and great grandchildren who lives in Vietnam, Sweden, France, U.S. and Canada. My father has four brothers and three sisters who lives in Vietnam and U.S.A. as well. My two sisters with their families are in Vietnam now, and one other sister and her family is in Sweden, and four brothers, one of my first elder brother with his family is in Vietnam, two brothers died for our country in the Vietnam War, and I have one little brother who lives with his family with a child and my mother in Vancouver, Canada. We were very close, even after my brothers and sisters got married, because we all were living in the same city, and visited each other frequently. Likewise, the neighbors found time to relax with friends and sometimes helped each other. Even today, we do this.

I graduated from Dong-Duc senior high school in both Vietnamese and Chinese languages. When I turned eighteen in 1972, I was supposed to enter military training, since military service was required because of the war. Yet, I did not want to be a fighter; therefore, I had to flee from Saigon to Tuy Hoa City (north of Saigon). Around that time when the war between North Vietnam and South Vietnam was heating up, and South Vietnam was drafting all the available young men who served in the army and navy.

From my point of view, I had been seeing more young men who were captured and constrained to the military service by the old regime government force. As a result, the new military obtained only shortly for the term to learn about the military program and they lacked of adequate military training, but hurried them straight to the war. By that time, not only were young men killed and wounded, but they were also deprived of their families and relatives. Not many returned home from the battlefield or when they came back, they were often crippled or disabled. We often lamented relatives and friends who had died in the war—as if life were only a dream of woe!

X

The unique photo of me as a baby. I was about a year and a half old, sitting on my mother's lap, taken at a photo studio in Cholon, Vietnam. ⇨

This is the last photo of my father and me together on my mother's birthday. 19 days after my father passed away on August 01, 2002.

XI

*My parents both were born in the Fukien part of China.
My father:* **Ta-Thanh-Ha**, *left China in 1920 when he was five, and my mother:*
Lac Thuat, *also left China in 1934 when she was eighteen. On the ground in a
pinch in China while living under the Communist force although they had
wealthy and good lives. They both have been through the World War I, and the
World War II, and the Vietnam War til Saigon's fall, and finally I sponsored them
to come to Canada after escaping from Vietnam.*

XII

This is me and my third sister on our balcony when I was about thirteen years old.

From right to left: me, my second youngest brother, my youngest brother, and our neighbor fellow.

XIII

*This is a picture of us and our relatives
from Sweden to Vancouver Airport, in B.C. Canada 1999.*

This is a picture of our family in Vancouver, B.C. Canada.

XIV

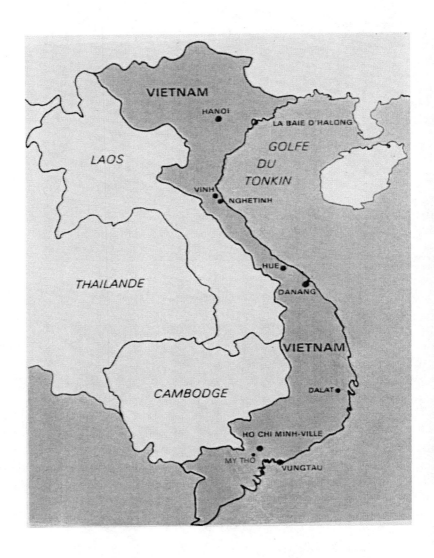

Introduction

*V*ietnam is a S-shaped nation bordered strategically by the South China Sea on the east and south, with a coastline stretching 3,000 kilometers. Laos and Kampuchea lie west of Vietnam. Vietnam's two biggest rice bowls are located in the Red River Delta and the Mekong River Delta. The Red and the Mekong Rivers, which are the richest rivers in the region, both flow through the country. This beautiful part of Vietnam's highlands is hilly or mountainous with rain forests going down to the sea. Seashores through along the coast plains and in the deltas of the Red and the Mekong Rivers. Therefore, over half of the South Vietnamese live in the Center Highlands through the Mekong River of the Coastal Lowlands for the essential agricultural development. The Vietnamese so-called carrying pole (don ganh) that connects the deltas as two rice baskets hanging from opposite ends; each rice basket shows that it comes from a farm to the market.

The city of Saigon (The city was originally named Saigon but was renamed Ho Chi Minh City after the fall of Saigon in 1975) is located in the south and is the largest city in Vietnam. The city of Hanoi in the north is Vietnam's second largest city. Hanoi is the center of government and Saigon is the central commerce. Other major cities are Hai-Phong, Hue, Da-Nang, Qui-Nhon, and Nha-Trang.

When the Vietnam War ended in 1975, South Vietnam was administratively divided into 44 provinces and 11 autonomous cities: Hue, Da-Nang, Qui-Nhon, Nha-trang, Cam-ranh, Vung-Tau, Da-Lat, My-Tho, Can-Tho, Rach-Gia, and capital city of Saigon. Also, Ha-Noi, Hai-Phong, and Ho-Chi-Minh City (Saigon) are designated as municipalities. The population of Saigon is more than 4 million, and the population of Ha-Noi is about 3.5 million. The population of Vietnam is more than 75 million. This S-shaped country contains 331,685 square kilometers.

Climate in South and North Vietnam

Vietnam's climate is totally tropical, but the weather conditions are different in the various regions. In the South, there are two main seasons: the wet and the dry. In Saigon, the wet seasons are from April to November, it brings slightly seasonal winds, and there is more rain falls in summer from the southwest 25 degrees Celsius to 32 degrees Celsius. The dry months are from January to March; when the temperatures can reach 32 degrees Celsius, it has a little rain, but when the winter monsoons blow in from the northeast Central Vietnam is cooler. The average daily temperature is 21 degrees Celsius. Some areas of the far north have four seasons. Between July and November, the violent typhoons often strike in from the

South China Sea and they often cause flooding and damage in the central coastal plains, where they destroys crops and damage homes.

Major Products in Vietnam

Most of the people in Vietnam are farmers and fishers.

"Rice" has long been the basic food in the country; Vietnamese grow rice fields in villages on the coastal deltas by rivers. Thousands of Vietnamese people who live along the coastline and numerous lakes and rivers to catch fish for a living and harvest forest products. Also, Vietnam is rich in natural resources from the mining and the manufacture such as oil, bauxite, phosphates, coal, iron, steel, lead, zinc, tin, wolfram, kaolin, limestone, cement and fertilizer and textile industries.

Vietnamese people raise livestock, and fish to earn their living because there is legal selling and buying of their produces in the open free market. Other products include tropical fruits and herbs, vegetables, potatoes, bananas, sugar canes, coffee and tea, coconuts, corn, peanuts, fish sauce, shrimp sauce, soybeans, salt, and tobacco.

Vietnamese History

Once upon a time, about 4000 years ago, the history of Vietnam began with the first "Viet" native, who was the dragon Lord named **Lac, Long Quang,** the ancestor of the Vietnamese. After Lac, Long Quang got married to the fairy **Au Co,** and had one hundred sons. Soon, each of the parents took fifty of their sons. One traveled east and stopped along the seacoast and on the lush meadows farm crops, and the other one traveled west and went to the mountain forests to live. Then Lac, Long Quang chose one of his sons to take over his kingdom. One of the sons Hung Vuong known as Van Lang, who was the first of eighteen kings, taught his people how to cultivate land and irrigate fertile. Van Lang became the first of the Hung dynasty in Vietnam according to mythology.

The Vietnamese is not only one group, all of whom are believed to have lived long ago in southern China and through to the Red River Delta in the northern Vietnam. These people later moved to the central high plateaus of the south. They met the Cham, the Khmer, they married each other. After Chinese frequently conquered northern Vietnam in the second century B.C. The Chinese changed the name to *An-Nam* (meaning pacified south), until the A.D. 938. The Chinese were finally defeated and expelled by Ngo Quyen. There were eleven dynasties that ruled in Vietnam until 1945.

The Chinese have not been the only invaders, but also Mongols, Indians, Portuguese, British, Japanese, French, Germany and Americans have all fought to control Vietnam. Finally, the Vietnamese set up an independent state. Although Vietnam remained independent, the history of this period was still troubled by the Chams, Khmers, the native tribes, and Chinese, lasting until the arrival of the French in the seventeenth century. Between 1859 and 1862, the French took over control the Saigon and Mekong River Delta, and they attacked North Hanoi, the Tonkin region, Annam of Central Vietnam and Cochin China of southern Vietnam in 1883, dividing Vietnam into three areas in order to govern the areas as separate parts of French Indochina, which also included Cambodia and Laos.

From 1941 to 1945 Japan controlled Vietnam during W W II. Then in March 1945, the Japanese stopped French troops and installed Emperor Bao Dai as nominal ruler, and the Japanese declared Vietnam as an " Independent " nation. Vietnam remained under the Japanese control until Japan and Germany were defeated in August 1945. When the Emperor Bao Dai abdicated, Ho Chi Minh (a Vietnamese Communist of north Hanoi) announced Vietnam's independence on September 02, 1945. Thus, the head <u>Ho</u> established the new government, which was caused by the Communist Vietminh, which formed the Democratic Republic of Vietnam in Hanoi.

The *Vietminh War* (a group controlled by Communists and headed by Ho Chi Minh in northern Vietnam), began in 1946, they attacked the French troops in Hanoi, and the *Indochina War* for eight-years. After World War II, the French troops returned to Vietnam with Communist and Nationalist forces. Although the Vietnamese emperor stayed on his throne, it was under French rules. It was a long war, when the Vietminh defeated the French in the battle of Dien-Bien-Phu was finally ended on May 07, 1954. A peace talk at the Geneva Conference decided to divide Vietnam temporarily into two parts of nations: Chairman Ho Chi Minh and Vietminh controlled the "Democratic Republic of Vietnam" (DRV), Vietnamese spelling, *Cong-Hoa Dan-Chu Viet-Nam,* in the north, or North Vietnam. France and President Ngo Dinh Diem controlled " The Republic of Vietnam ", Vietnamese spelling, *Viet-Nam Cong-Hoa,* in the south, or South Vietnam. After the fall of Saigon in 1975 renamed "The Socialist Republic of Vietnam", Vietnamese spelling, *Cong-Hoa Xa-Hoi Chu-Nghia Viet-Nam.*

The Viet History repeated the show, when the Vietnam War began in 1957. A member of the *Viet-Cong* (a guerrilla band in south Vietnamese supported for Vietminh known as the National Liberation force from North Vietnam) rebelled against the South Vietnamese government, and then the fighting grew larger, becoming the Vietnam Civil War. Both

North and South Vietnam broke out the war in 1959, then the French were gone and the United States were getting involved in Vietnam War. The Vietnam Civil War, the conflict between North Vietnam and South Vietnam lasted for about thirty years, from 1945 to 1975. Many people were against **communism**, they supported the United States of whom supported South Vietnam. While North Vietnam was aided by the People's Republic of China and the Soviet Union.

Vietnamese Language, Cultural, Education and Religions

The official language is all in Vietnamese. Most Vietnamese is spoken from different regions, because they have their own distinctive accents, mixed origins, and speech habits from some of the dialects. At school, many scholars choose to speak French or English as a second language, and than Chinese, and Japanese; other languages include Khmer and various tribal languages in the rural. The different ethnic groups in Vietnam use at least fifty different dialects. The most popular languages in these minorities groups include the hill tribes and Montagnards or Highlanders. They used to speak French or English because of the French and Americans against the Vietminh in Hanoi. Members of these hill tribes also speak their native dialect, such as Cham, Mon-

Khmer, Tai-Kadai and Sino-Tibetan, Tay, Nung, Tai, Muong and Hmong. They live in the Southeast Asian archipelago, and in the central high plateaus of the southwest from the northern provinces.

The Chinese who first settled in the North Vietnam over 2000 years ago, made their home from north of the Red River Delta and to the southern Mekong River Delta where they carried on small businesses; therefore, Chinese were quick to capitalize and mainly strong control economic all trades of marketplaces in the Cholon district of Ho Chi Minh City.

There were many Vietnamese who married Chinese or cultivated friendship with each other, creating a community that spoke both Vietnamese and Chinese dialects such as *Cantonese, Fukien*, and *Chaozhu languages.* Moreover, many Vietnamese people learned about *Confucius* from the Chinese settlers. Confucius was a founder of educationalist was a teacher and philosopher living in China, and Confucianism was introduced to Vietnam over 2000 years ago. Most of the Vietnamese people are Buddhists. Other religions in Vietnam include Taoism, Cao Dai, Hoa Hao, Roman Catholicism, Moslems, and Hindus. These religions are still practiced by some Vietnamese.

Through the centuries of the life, many of the descendants of

Chinese Vietnamese feared of reprisals by a Communist government, and therefore they fled the country after the Vietnam War ended in 1975.

Vietnam Life in Saigon and Cholon — Ho Chi Minh City

Saigon and Cholon—as the local's people still call it, is reunification in 1975, now called Ho Chi Minh City the capital of South Vietnam.

Saigon and Cholon City are the commercial hearts of Vietnam and they possess many attractions, such as Art, Military, and National History museums, as well as theatres, religions, the Parks, Zoos, and Botanical Gardens, etc.

The city has 14 districts but most areas of interest are in either District 1 or 2, which is called downtown Saigon. The major building and arteries are Le Loi and Nguyen Hue Boulevards, and Dong Khoi street (Tu Do street). The largest Saigon markets and Cho Ben-Thanh are in the center of downtown Saigon. Hotels include the Rex, the Caravelle and Continental. The Opera House, and similar style public buildings were built by the French and made famous during the Vietnam War.

Districts 5 and 6 are called Cholon–Chinatown; comprising several kilometers southwest of downtown Saigon. The major buildings and arteries of Cholon are Thap-Muoi, Tran-Hung-Dao, Nguyen-Tri-Phuong, and Dong- Khanh Boulevards. On Hau-Giang Boulevard, is the large Binh - Tay market place, and Cho-Lon Moi, are bustling with people and activities. In Cholon and Saigon, the houses are crowded together wall to wall, the house are made of stucco, bricks, cement, and are used for building materials with tiled roofs. In rural places houses are built from simple wood or bamboo, with roofs made of palm leaves or straw; but in Hanoi, many houses and buildings are near run-down since the French built in the late 1800's. In Cholon, this city is the largest ethnic Chinese community in Vietnam, and most important businesses in the economy operate in this bustling Chinatown; therefore, Cholon, was formerly a separate sister city, but now hundreds of thousands of Chinese have left Vietnam because fear of government persecution, causing the area to lose much of its traditional Chinese character, and their economical power control as well.

The main aspect of Saigon and Cholon streets are bustling and filled with motorcycles while the whole family is squeezed on seat. There are also bicycles, cyclomobile, and cyclos (pedicabs), lambretas (tiny three wheeled vehicles), autobus, taxis, trucks and a few automobiles at day and night.

The streets, markets, and restaurants are scenes of noisy animation, and the sidewalks are home to a starting range of much activity. In particular, we saw so often in Vietnam that women are dressed in costumes (ao dai), Vietnamese tradition as costumes, which are very colorful on a black or white smock-like pullover, consists of a long sleeved blouse with a high neckline, and a high-heeled wooden sandals (guoc) were worn with the ao dai, this is a special part of every woman's wardrobe, and for their popular occasions, they wear a conical hat (non la), which is made from straw or palm, which was used to protect them from the heat of the sun and rain, to school or market. Men are dressed in traditional suits (ao the), coat-like pullover that hangs to their knees, and the tunic in looser, and wear shoes for their particular days as well. By and large, men mostly wear loose fitting pants that are plain and long or short-sleeved T-shirts and jeans. Now, it is common to see both Vietnamese females and males wear Western-style clothing in the cities. But between northern and southern Vietnam the clothing styles are different from each other's.

In Saigon, and Cholon City , you can find all kinds of souvenirs all around. Most of these souvenirs are handmade objects such as woodcarvings; lacquer ware, silk paintings, ceramics, vases and furniture all are tradition style productions. And also you can crowed into any a café stands, noodle stalls, indoors " Pho " shops. The **Pho** contains rice noodle with beef broth cinnamon, ginger, small slices of beef or chicken meat with tasty hot and spicy or dried chili and mint leaves, this is the most common and favorite food in Vietnam. Usually I make *Pho* and *spring rolls* at home in Canada, because those are my favorite Vietnamese foods!

These are some of the Vietnamese foods that are mixtures of French style: Chicken salad (Goi ga), Port Pate (Cha lua), Spring rolls (Cha gio), a steam rice pancake (Banh cuon), sour soup (Canh chua), and Fish sauce (Nuoc mam) used for dipping is on the menu eaten at tables and wooden benches. A hundred other such items are foods and drinks in bamboo baskets balanced on poles over venders' shoulders. At the teeming markets they sale a wide variety of fresh tropical fruits, and vegetables from the farm. Fresh seafood and meat are produced daily; consequently, people there never look for frozen foods.

*Sun-rise at **Ha-Long Bay**, North of Ha-Noi, Vietnam.*
*[Photograph by **Mae Seto Quan**]*

*Sun-set at **Ha-Long Bay**, North of Ha-Noi, Vietnam.*
*[Photograph by **Mae Seto Quan**]*

In cities of Vietnam, many women still wear the traditional Vietnamese ao dai (a long coat-like garment)
*[Photograph by **Ly, Thuong Lam**]*

The large Binh Tay market place in Cholon, Vietnam.
*[Photograph by **Ly, Thuong Lam**]*

The largest Saigon market — Ben Thank market place in the center of downtown Saigon, Vietnam.
*[Photograph by **Ly, Thuong Lam**]*

National History Museum (Saigon's Zoo), and Botanical Garden in Saigon Vietnam. *[Photograph by **Ly, Thuong Lam**]*

17

Motorcycles, bicycles, cyclos in a bustling day in Saigon, Cholon, Vietnam.
*[Photograph by **Ly, Thuong Lam**]*

*... While family is squeezed on one seat [Photograph by **Ly, Thuong Lam**]*

Vietnam's largest city, are crowed with peddlers or vendors, they are display their produce on the sidewalks in front of stores and house.
[Photograph by **Ly, Thuong Lam**]

19

Women selling food and drinks from bamboo baskets balanced on poles over their shoulders in South and North Vietnam.

*[Photograph by **Mae Seto Quan**]*

A Favorite Part of Vung-Tau Beach

Vung-Tau, is the most popular beach resort in the south. Also, the Vung-Tau's largest beach, known as the *Bay of Boats*–is located on a peninsula 125 kilometers southeast of Saigon City. It is on a coastal and mountainous district with beautiful scenery and a stretch of beach. There are restaurants, café shops, gift shops, markets and other facilities, and colonial villas for tourism all year round. It is need to take a trip organize to see seacoast life there.

When I was living in Cholon, I was only too pleased to visit Vung-Tau resort and beach with my family outing for seaside walking, and relaxing on a weekend and holidays. When I was there I took a great delight of picking seashells, watching seabirds, and looking at the sea. It is also a pleasant to hear the waves. I always enjoyed the sea scenery while eating in a seafood house along the coast, under the genial sun, and when the windy breeze blew in my face it felt really pleasant. Likewise, I was very fond of mountaineering, sometimes climbing up to the top of mountain to see the superb view over Vung-Tau. From there, I enjoyed taking pictures. I was really fond of roaming and forgot to return home. There! On the mountain top of Vung-Tau Beach is a huge Bodhisattva (Bo Tat); people worship it and pay homage to the Buddha!

Our family members visited Vung Tau in 1970, picture taken in front of the huge Bodhisattva statue. From left back row: Phat (my nephew), my sister, my mon, and from front row: My (my niece), Duc (my nephew)

The largest beach—Vung Tau Bay of Boats from south-east of Saigon City. From middle front row : Johnny (myself), on the right front my dad 1970.

The Vietnam War in 1968

One of my strongest early memories is *the Vietnam War in 1968*. When I was fourteen years old.

Since early 1968, South Vietnam and North Vietnam had a desperate hyper-fight; therefore, many of young men were forced to train for the war, and go to war against the enemies at the front line. During this time, many young men escaped military service by cutting off their fingers, blinding themselves, pretending to be monks, or even bribed officers in order to not go frontline.

The country was undergoing a convulsion and political in 1968. The **Tet** (which means the Vietnam celebration for new year, the year of the *"monkey"*, 1968) offensive erupted throughout South Vietnam on January 30, 1968 while the Vietcong was destroying major cities of South Vietnam's capital and in Hue province. The fighting and the horror was widened by Communist atrocities. The Vietcong's strategy decimated much of the population including massacres of civilians: they were upward of 38,000 killed and 6900 captured. The Vietnamese people on both side of the war suffered almost close to 5 million deaths.

The weapons and warfare techniques used by the Vietcong included booby traps, bows and arrows. This device was used by aboriginal tribes to kill animals but was adapted by Viet Cong for use in the war. Many mines were set around a fallen tree or log lying across a track. The military equipment used by the Vietcong also included Chinese rifle and Soviet field gun, rocket launchers, and tanks.

The Civil War smoldered in the sky. There was an enormous slaughter between South Vietnamese and the Communist guerrillas and their rebellions massacred from the battle in the air and on the ground. The North Vietnamese massacred thousands of South and North Vietnamese soldiers, and millions of civilians were killed and became refugees. More than half the people of Vietnamese were left homeless. Bombs destroyed people, tearing them limb from limb. Vehicles broke down and iron lay in a litter was on the streets. This war kept on and on, time to time, year by year . . . My family and I fled from one canton to another canton of the district between Saigon and Cho-Lon. We had seen lots of aircraft bombing, such those carried out by the American B-52 bombers. When South Vietnam soldiers fought the Vietcong which was such a **Terror War,** the terrorists used bomber aircrafts, patrol planes, warships, cannon tanks, land mines, grenades, labrum bombs, and so on. All this burst into flames and the people burst into tears not far away from Saigon and Cholon!

My School Damaged in 1968

Before the war ended in 1975. I attended the original Fukien School (Phuoc-Duc School). It was built in 1907 for primary, senior and junior private school; the building is divided with three sections merging the whole building, the class's students are including an upward of fifteen thousands, and more than three hundred teachers before the fall of Saigon. After the war ended in 1975, it changed to Tran-Boi-Co School, address, 266 Khong-Tu Boulevard, now it is Tran-Boi-Co Street, in Cholon, District 5.

Phuoc-Duc School was my alma mater. In 1968, during the civil war between South and North Vietnam. The Phuoc-Duc School was one of the schools in center at Cholon that was used for urgent table meetings by the South Vietnamese army, so no classes were held. Meanwhile, the school area was terribly bombed by a South Vietnamese air force officer by mistake. The Vietcong also detonated bombs and explosives, they terrorized the crowded public places, like in the markets, theatres, schools, district offices, and community centers all around in Saigon and Cholon. People were injured and killed, and the structure was damaged, vehicles shattered on the streets, and tree limbs, as result that was the **Tet Offensive** erupted, hit up to one hundred cities and towns in South Vietnam, and the fighting lasted until late February, 1968.

*Before the war ended in 1975___the **Phuoc-Duc School** at 266 Khong-Tu Boulevard. District 5. Cholon, Vietnam.*

*After the war ended in 1975___the **Phuoc-Duc School** had changed to **Tran-Boi-Co School** by the government in HoChiMinh City.*

End of the War in Sight

Apparently, a delegation from the United States, North and South Vietnam, and the Vietcong (South Vietnamese rebels) held their first formal meeting in Paris on May 13, 1968. The "peace talks" were three days later, the Vietcong continued the combat and a massacre took place at My Lai on March 16, 1968 right after the *Tet Offensive,* and The Khe Sanh was finally abandoned on June 23, 1968.

On July 18 to 20, 1968, President Lyndon Johnson and President Nguyen Van Thieu met in Honolulu, and on October 31, 1968, President Lyndon Johnson announced that the bombing of North Vietnam would end the following day, although reconnaissance fights would continue. In November 1968, The President-elect Richard M Nixon promised a gradual troop withdraw from South Vietnam.

As for the Americans ground troops operated in Cambodia, Thai-Land, and Laos, the U.S. and Thai government announced in September 1969 to pull out American militaries from Thailand, and U.S. ground troops got withdraw from Cambodia by June 1970. In Laos, Americans supported Meo troops that were on the verge of defeat by North Vietnamese units in 1971. The North Vietnamese forces invaded South Vietnam on March 30, 1972, and Quang-Tri (north of Vietnam) fell to the North Vietnamese, so Quang-Tri province remained in the Communist hands on September 16, 1972.

The last U.S. ground combat troops left South Vietnam on March 29, 1973, but support personnel still remained. Two months later, the war broke out again. The Americans at home were very angry about the large loss of life in Vietnam, and families in the U.S.A. helped to convince the U.S. government to withdraw its soldiers and weapons from our country; therefore, no one American troops returned to the war in mid-1973. Still, in late 1974, North Vietnamese and the Vietcong troops attacked Phuoc-Long (northeast of Saigon), and early in April 1975, North Vietnamese forced and launched South Vietnamese troops to retreat in the Central Highlands. Finally, the U.S failed to come to the aid of South Vietnam and therefore the Vietnam War came to an abrupt end on April 30, 1975.

My Life in Tuy-Hoa — Phu-Yen

On the ground in the Vietnam War, I was on needles and pins with no resolutions in sight, so I left Saigon City in 1972 and went to Tuy-Hoa City, *the capital of Phu-Yen province,* which is about 280 kilometers north of Saigon, this is a nondescript little town on the coast between Dai-Land Beach and Qui-Nhon province. Tuy-Hoa was less strict about conscription. People of Tuy-Hoa were very friendly, helpful, social-able, and passionate. I used to learn and understand the people's dialect and their living while I was residing in Tuy-Hoa City. There, on this mountaintop with a high pagoda, was a relic of the Mongolian period. From there, the view from the mountain was grand. While I was in Tuy-Hoa City, I was a helper in a fabric store and I boarded in my surrogate uncle Nhan's home; he was my brother-in-law's friend since they knew each other in Saigon. Uncle Nhan was a businessman, who would buy fabrics in Saigon and sell them to Tuy-Hoa from his store where I earned my keep as a helper. Uncle and aunt Nhan were a kind humane couple, which liked having me around. I stayed with them for more than three years in Tuy-Hoa.

In the meantime, uncle Nhan let me borrow a certificate from his son **Nhan, Chi -Phuoc,** who was 16 years old. I used this birth paper as transient while I was staying in Tuy-Hoa City, and therefore I did not go to military service. Holding a namesake of Nhan,Chi-Phuoc, it seem that I knew someone by this name since I was in Saigon! . . . That is right! I recall this name; he was one of my classmates, whom we were attending in prep school for an English course in the Dieu Han senior high school, in Cholon. I could not believe my eyes when I asked uncle Nhan about that, for they told me that they have four sons who were living in Cholon, all attending school. One of their elder son's name is *Nhan Chi-Phuoc,* but he changed another name to be prepared for next two years if due to military service problem. In the beginning of summer, 1972, uncle Nhan's children came from Cholon to visit them in Tuy-Hoa. There! I had a great chance to meet my old classmate *Phuoc;* we met altogether at his parents' fabric store. Whence, in life, where do not people meet? Everything was mysterious for my life in TuyHoa!

One year later, I had to change one another identification for a younger age; consequently, I continued my education in Tuy-Hoa. There, I went to a police station and bought off an officer for an identification with a new name that was Ngo, Van-Sanh and to say that I was fifteen years old in order to try to evade military service. It worked and I did not have to go into the military during Vietnam Civil War.

Tuy-Hoa's panoramic view, Vietnam.

*Visiting my principle **Thich Dong Tien**. Photo taken in front of the **Chua Bao Tinh** as **The Unification of Vietnamese Budhist Temple** in the province of Phu-Yen, in 1974.*

*This picture of me was taken at the tower of **Chua Bao Tinh Temple**
Tuy-Hoa __ Phu-Yen
June 1974.*

My Return to Saigon

In 1975, I returned to Saigon City to visit my parents, brothers, sisters, friends, and other relatives. I went there to celebrate the Lunar New Year, and I ended up living there for two months in my sister's and parents' home, although I had planned to go back to Tuy-Hoa City, because it was safer and less strict there. I had a good visit through the following fall of Saigon till I escaped from the country in 1979.

Returning to Saigon, I visited a pen pal girl with whom I had been exchanging letters for about three years since I was living in the town of Tuy-Hoa. It was so wonderful to me to have that great opportunity to meet together in Cholon while it was the New Year of February 1975. Since then we had a lot of dates in Saigon and Cholon. Yet, we met til 1978. This was my first time in my life to meet her, we fell head over heals with each other at first sight.

Following the fall of Saigon, we were among the many " boat people " who fled Vietnam. However, a circumstance changed me to have to flee from Vietnam; therefore, I had to say "so long " my girlfriend, but I promised her that I would sponsor her after landing a third country. Finally, I left Saigon before her, and she planned to escape later. These events, were like "bringing the dead back to life". She crossed from

Hanoi to China, and sailed to Hong Kong, I suffered from pirates for fifteen days while sailing to Indonesia. By the way, we also kept contact by writing letters for each other, even though we were both far away between two different refugee camps.

I settled in Canada in March 1980. As soon as possible I put an application for her to come as a landing immigrant, and it was granted. Just a few months sooner, she arrived at Vancouver, Canada with me. We got married within three months after she landed. I am the father of two; both are boys (Edward & Brian). Sadly, in 1986, our marriage life broke up. I tried to forget it, but it was difficult for me in that period of the time. Time passed, I believe it was my fate so I had to accept it. As luck would have it!

After four years later, I met a pen pal girl in 1990. Wendy, who is my wife now, she came from Macao, landed in Hawaii. We had a long honeymoon across Canada and United States. We will continue to Asia, and Europe for the honeymoon in the fiscal years. Wendy cares for the family more, she is an intelligent housewife, and hence I love her very deeply. Yes! We are happily married to live together forever since we were married to each other, and I am father of two, they are one boy and girl (Jay & Kay), so I am father of four now. They are all attending school.

Our wedding pictures taken in 1990

Our Family pictures taken at home in Vancouver, Canada.

Vietnam War North and South

By that time the U.S. began the gradual withdrawal of their combat troops, and aircraft carriers from Vietnam because the peace talks had failed and the enemy continued scheming for a frightful slaughter in South Vietnam. President Richard M. Nixon did not want involvement in the conflict while meeting at Midway Island with President Nguyen Van Thieu. By this policy, known as *Vietnamization,* Nixon reduced the huge number of American combat troops from South Vietnam. On September 04, 1969, Radio Hanoi announced the death of Ho Chi Minh. At this time, there was an important change in the war between North and South Vietnam.

On April 01, 1975, as President Lon Noi fled Cambodia, fierce battles occurred between Cambodia, which had fallen to the Communist insurgents on April 17, and Laos's government troops under the Pathet Lao, Communists that took over Laos on August 23, 1975. The Ambassador to Cambodia and his staff leave Phnom Penh on April 12, 1975.

Between March 1975 and April 30, 1975, the North Communist insurgents and the South Vietnamese troops fought fiercely. During this heavy fighting the Communist of the north captured Xuan-Loc, which is about sixty-four kilometers east of Saigon. Later, a very costly part of the war was battled in Ban Me Thuat located in the Central Highlands. This is about hundred fifty kilometers northeast of Saigon. Pleiku and Kon-tum, located in central Vietnam, were abandoned; so mainly the Vietcong guerrilla forces — a group was known as Vietminh, and still the Vietnamese Communist Party was controlling the war.

The Vietcong and Vietminh went on a long Vietnam War, and the Vietnamese people on both sides were forced to suffer more than five million deaths and people risked their lives under the Communist force. The United States became the chief ally of the South in which the United States' comrade-in-arms took part and participated in the Vietnam War, which started in 1957 and ended in 1975. All and all, we, the Vietnamese and the Overseas Vietnamese realize that such violent killing was doing wrong and extremely bad!

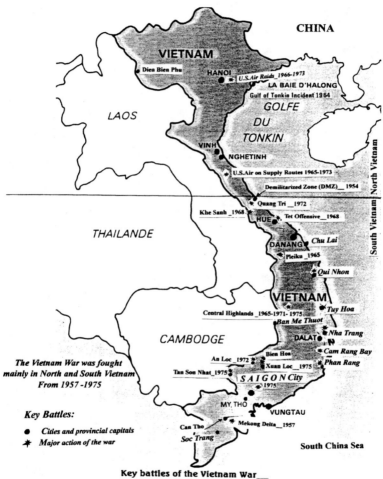

Key battles of the Vietnam War
It began in 1957 to 1975

Lambreta 550 • *The Lambreta 550 was used by the Communist soldiers for carrying trinitrotoluene "TNT", guns AK47 from suburban to Saigon, these weapons were used in the Tet general offensive in 1968.*

The Renault • *The Renault was used to transport the Communist wounded soldiers and cadres from Co-Gap district to Cu-Chi district in the Tet general offensive in 1968.*

Simca • *The Simca was used to collect communist to carry **medical equipments** and weapons from Cu-Chi to urban city in 1955 to 1972*
*[Photograph by **Ly, Thuong Lam**]*

Peugeot 403 • *The Peugeot 403 was used to take the comrade **Vo-Van-Kiet**, the secretary of Saigon Gia-Dinh committee urban city to nearby provinces to lead the revolutionary movements in 1962 to 1975*
*[Photograph by **Ly, Thuong Lam**]*

On April 08, 1975, the Communist soldiers used the Fighter F5 dropped two bombs which hit the Independence Palace (The Presidential Palace in Saigon, Vietnam).

On April 28, 1975, the Communist soldiers seized the Fighter A37 from South Vietnamese soldiers taking off from Phan-Rang airport to attack Saigon, Tan-Son-Nhot airport, destroyed 28 aircrafts and quit off line of American current military assistant.

*[Photograph by **Ly, Thuong Lam**]*

The Vietnam War in 1975

In my reminiscence, a second principle event occurred in April 1975.

After the American troops left South Vietnam it ended on March 29, 1973, the Communist launched a very large offensive against South Vietnam, then, the fight was going on and on . . . . . . During this time, the South Vietnam's government commanded a large group of uniformed police and plain clothes detectives to come to knock on doors day and night to enter or burst into houses, sometimes not even knocking, to check and catch any man from seventeen to fifty-eight years old, so they could conscript them recruitment training and mobilization into the army and navy crops, and second reserve, but some were enrolled in the troops. Those were desperate days in 1975. On the April 21, 1975. President Nguyen Van Thieu resigned and gave General Duong Van Minh, who helped overthrow the President Ngo Dinh Diem in 1963, the power to rule temporarily as president of South Vietnam.

Thousands of South Vietnam civilians fled, and many South Vietnam soldiers were killed accidentally in events of battles.

Because of this the South Vietnamese people lobbied the government to end the war. Even though South Vietnam agreed to peace, North Vietnam ignored the agreement and continued to fight. Finally, Americans became impatient for the war to end.

The Fall of Saigon

Just months before we faced the unrelenting firing power of the North Vietnamese troops. The evening of the April 29, 1975, the North Communist infantry and insurgents used surprise attacks to overcome the South Vietnamese. Although the President Gerald R. Ford, and Nixon's successor asked Congress for $700 million in military to provide the army of the Republic of South Vietnam with the best American weapons helped the frontline, Congress provided less than half in emergency aids because the war was receiving U.S. support.

After the last Americans fled Vietnam in helicopters landing on the top roof of the old United States Embassy in Saigon on April 30, 1975, and a few of the American's marines and airfields were hurrying to get lifted by helicopters. Other Americans and many of their South Vietnamese allies were evacuated just before abandoning the city to South Vietnam's patriot for their country.

In the aftermath, the American troops had been engaged in a futile war they did not win. Without much aid from Western countries, millions of people in Indochina may be deprived of the fortune, freedom and a better life.

War Ends April 30, 1975

Lastly, the Vietnam War ended in the afternoon of April 30, 1975, at 12:15 pm.

Early in the morning, the North revolutionary soldiers and their guerrilla thrust to the coast and down to Vietcong cadres, who steered their Russian-made tanks into the street of Saigon. The Vietcong smashed down the gate of the Presidential Palace, and even hit Tan-Son-Nhot airfield. On April 30, 1975, the first two tanks of the tank brigade 203 attacked and took over the Presidential Palace, and another tank crashed through the main wrought iron gates, they ripped the yellow flag with the three red stripes off, and pulled the revolutionary flag, the red and blue flag with a golden star in the center, up to the top of the palace at 11:30a.m. President Minh announced South Vietnam's unconditional surrender shortly after on the radio at 12:15p.m on April 30, 1975, and then the revolutionary flag was hoisted all over the city. The flags and the banners rippled and rose all over all of South Vietnam's forty-four provinces.

I was at home in the meantime; walking to and fro in the front and back yard waiting to receive news from the radio, while I heard terrible gun fires coming from the air in the city where I lived, then civilians including children were yelling, crying, and running crazily on the streets sites for fleeing the scene of combat. I saw far away in the black sky smoke and fire, the vehicles were blocking the roads and the cyclos, and bicycles were rushing quickly. The venders hurried and packed their food items and rushed home. Alleys that were narrow and small were filled with many people running around the crowded place. During that time I was so worried that I forgot to eat my meals; I only remembered to drink a few cups of water. My family who were right beside me were worried as well. Besides, we already packed all our special needs in case we needed to evade quickly to a safe place to stay away from the fighting and explosions.

Later in the afternoon, the gunfire's gradually began to stop and I felt very glad. I believed that my feeling was the same as all of the people who had traveled over the deep blue sea, and thousands upon thousands of loving and peaceful of Vietnam. Although it made peace with our lives, it is under Communist force. On second thoughts Vietnam Communist seemed to be in "peace", but the fact is, there were many hardships for people who lived in South Vietnam while the Communist controlled people in the first ten decade.

The next day was the International Workers' Day—May 01, the main event of Labor Day, the people of South Vietnam were saddened by the North's military parades all over the whole nation.

As a result of the Vietnam War, about fifty-eight thousand Americans died, and an estimated of more than three hundred thousand were wounded. South Vietnamese deaths were about one million, and North Vietnamese lost a range of direct war about five hundred thousands and one million. A large number of civilians in North and South Vietnam were killed.

The Continuing Conflict Troubles on Their Way

The Vietnam War ended, but the Vietnamese Communists invaded Cambodia (now renamed Kampuchea) while the Khmer Rouge was backed up by China. This was fought by China and Vietnam near the border between these two countries on February 17, 1979. The Chinese troops counterattacked and destroyed six provinces that included damaged houses and burned crop fields. This was done to "punish" and "teach" the Vietnamese a lesson. The Chinese troops seized Tran Dong Dang in Langson and Bangioc Fall in Caobang (near Hanoi). Finally, China announced that its troops withdrew on March 16, 1979, as they only wanted peace from the Vietnamese aggressors.

48

South Vietnam's President **Duong-Van-Minh** announced
unconditional surrender to the revolutionary soldiers
at The Voice of Saigon Vietnamese radio broadcast
station, and the long war ended on April 30, 1975.
(Seated in front of the microphone is President Duong-Van-Minh)
[The above picture is photo copied from Ho So Interpol
#174 RA 27/04/2000.]

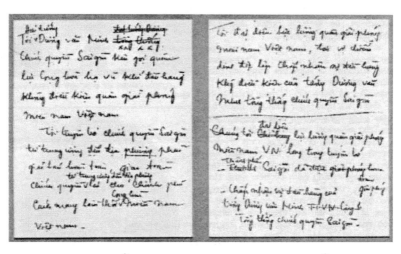

(Left) ↑   **(Right)** ↑

*From (left), a draft of agreement from the President **Duong-Van-Minh** announcing unconditional surrender to the revolutionary soldiers. The Vietnam War ended on April 30, 1975, at 12:15 p.m.*
*From (right), a draft of agreement from the revolutionary soldiers that accepted the announcement about unconditional surrender from the President **Duong-Van-Minh**.*
[The avove picture is photo copied from a Vietnamese Newspaper # 174 RA 27/04/2000.]

The Unification Palace, (The Presidential Palace "Dinh Doc Lap",
known as Independence Palace) in Saigon City, South Vietnam.
[This is a copied picture from a Vietnamese
tourist handbook #184/VHTT 24/04/2000.]

The tank 843 attacked and took over **The Presidential Palace**
in South Vietnam's Saigon, the war ended on April 30, 1975.
[VNA/courtesy John Spragens, Jr]

Citizens Forced by Communists

During the infancy of the liberation, following the fall of Saigon in 1975, there were many rumors in the air that a lot of agitators incited the rebellion. For all that, people's living became expensive, perilous, and fearsome under these circumstances.

The war was over. The North Vietnamese brought in the Communist system and widely enforced it. During the years between 1975 and 1978, the government gained strict control to all of South Vietnam's social programs to make a move to the whole thousand, up to tens of thousands people from cities to rural areas were facing a poor economical development, because of overcrowding and unemployment in the urban, but as it was, this plan was carried out! *Because of living under Communist rule*, there was not much need for a trade market system like before. Gradually, the people became poor and did not have enough food even though they were forced to work harder. Indeed, up to four hundred thousands of southern citizens, including civil servants, intellectuals, artisans, business merchants, and south soldiers surrendered and were imprisoned in **political re-education camps** for five to twenty four years behind bars. Millions of people were also forcibly relocated, and put people through hell, into **new economical zones** as their backgrounds.

Moreover, young people were brainwashed at school, and the adults were forced to attend meetings three times a week to be brainwashed into the Communist's system.

Today, people in Vietnam do not have basic rights such as freedom of assembly, freedom of press, freedom to worship, freedom to travel, the right to have family, the right to reside at a certain location, and the right to earn a living. The Communist also deprived families or relatives of those held in concentration **camps** or those of **suspected class** of basic rights and freedoms, In short, the people of Vietnam lack democracy.

Money Available Under Communists

Between 1975 and 1978, the Vietnamese Communist government secretly changed the currency from the South Vietnam **dong** (piaster) to the new political system's dong. They made only a limited amount for each numbered account in the national bank. Consequently many rich people and merchants had reduced a number of dong in their accounts.

However, the rich people would transfer money to their relatives or to their friends' accounts: they could trust them. They would keep some money or merchandise in their homes secretly in storage and for the inventory in the near future.

During this period the government frequently changed the national currency. The new government would suddenly change money orders during the curfew or martial law on a certain day. They also conducted home visits to register people's capital, current assets, and other immovable things by providing people substitute vouchers by the Communist staff or the revolution army, so a man of any substance could not remove or transfer their money in any way. Also, many millionaires had to destroy or burn their money; otherwise, they would be convicted of an offence.

Life Under Communism Compared to "Capitalism"

Nevertheless, the Communists in Vietnam controlled the assets of <u>the great classes,</u> <u>the middle classes</u> and <u>the low classes</u>. They imposed the totalitarian and repressive regime first to the previous "bourgeois", and then the "capitalists" after the end of Vietnam War in 1975.

In point of the facts, the former capitalists, and bourgeois were forced to become classless. Also, they were forced to leave their homeland and were forced to construct ditches and roads (forced labor) into the wilderness under the names of <u>new economic zones,</u> and <u>hard labor camps.</u> Then, their assets were taken under the Communist's totalitarian rule. Hundreds and thousands of people were sent to the infamous

<u>re-education camps</u> to be "brainwashed" under the Communist regime system.

As a matter of fact, all merchandise and industrial companies were nationalized. The government controlled even **Co-operative Societies and Services;** therefore, all manufacturing and production were operated by the government.

The Black Market

As a result, the market price of commodities soared and rocketed each day and month. For example, staple goods and foods necessary for life were in short supply in stores. As matter of course, there were lots of adulterated faulty, and stolen goods or contra-banded goods such as drug use from marijuana, cocaine, and heroin, which spread quickly in the Vietnamese markets. Local citizens were able to buy and sell these things, where they needed and got them from the North Vietnamese comrades who went with the stream at black market prices. This of course was done privately.

In short, corner markets have appeared all around Saigon, Cholon, and other cities wherever possible. Doubtless, other business and marketing was inactive and dull after the end of the war in 1975.

Small Shops Appearing

As matter of fact, in order for my family to survive, my parents and I first operated a noodle stand between our house and our sister's. It was in front of her house because it was a good location. This lasted for a year since the fall of Saigon.

Later, we changed businesses from the noodle stand and opened a small retail grocery store at the same locations. This also lasted for over a year.

By 1977, early in the summer, the Regional Vietnamese cadres came to register our business. They sealed all of our merchandise in bags, yet they tried to confiscate our goods. I was angry about it; I came up to their local office to met one of the officers. I explained my situation. A couple of months later, we resumed our business. This happened because we were not considered to belong to any class. So, we were not considered or on listed to mark to be *capitalists* since they wanted to control our assets and dissolve peddlers all hawkers in the town and city like Saigon, Cholon, and other centers.

Early in 1978, my way of life changed to work in a Ping Pong Paddle Product Factory cooperating with nationalized local businesses. We had fifteen members to invest in this business which was also under the local Communist control. This was recommended from my nephew **Ly, Tuyen-Phat**'s friend's parents, so we got down to business. Phat's friend was the direct Manager, Phat was a vice Manager of the producer. My niece, **Ly, Ngoc-Anh** was the Secretary, and **Ly, Ngoc-Buu** was the Special Inspector for the production and Supervisor. Myself, I was an Accountant for the Finance Systems. I began a year later, the business was going to pour in because of the lack of adequate for materials; as the Vietnam businesses fell in as behind for economic change, we had cut corners on production costs, but it drew a complete blank, and therefore we lost capital and closed down finally.

My Surrogate Uncle Nhan and Family Closed Their Store Under Communist's Force

My surrogate uncle Nhan, was a friend of my brother-in-law. Uncle Nhan was in the fabric business that drove a roaring trade! His business was named **Vinh -Tuyen- Hung** for many years in Tuy-Hoa City. Under the Communists, his assets were declared to be the *capitalist* in 1977. Under this situation, the reason that uncle Nhan changed his fabric business to a factory that produced "tires", was because his business was nationalized and operated by the local government. To avoid the government from taking over his business, so uncle Nhan closed the store and escaped from the

*My surrogate uncle **Nhan** and his wife visited us in Vancouver, Canada, 2000.*

country in December 1977. For all I knew, uncle and aunt Nhan and their children escaped as refugees to Hong Kong. They eventually re-settled to U.S.A. in 1978. Living for a while in Texas, both uncle and aunt had a grocery store for a living until 1997 for their retirements. In June 2000, we were very happy to have a visit from uncle and aunt Nhan and their children, including my classmate Phuoc; we met all in together in Vancouver after twenty-three years since we escaped from Saigon Vietnam. Uncle Nhan passed away in March 2001. Oh uncle Nhan, friends may meet, but mountains never greet!

My Brother-In-Law Forced Out of Business by Communists

My brother-in-law was the owner of the fabric retail and wholesale company and the trade was prosperous with a tail in the water! His business's name was **Tuyen-Tan-Phat** for also many years in Cholon. The control of his assets was seized by the Communist regime in 1977, because it was considered to him to be part of the *bourgeois*.

Finally, the Communists who nationalized the fabric store closed it. Meanwhile, my brother-in-law and sister were making plans to smuggle their children out of the country.

On the right is my borther-in-law and beside him is my sister who came to visit us in Vancouver, B.C., Canada, 1999.

My Brother-in-law in the center row with my sister, his family, my nieces and nephews and my grand nieces in Sweden.

My nephews and nieces escaped from Vietnam in 1979. They landed in Indonesia Island, then they re-settled in Sweden in 1980. After that, they sponsored their parents to go there in 1982. Their families are living happily now and have visited us in Canada four times since 1987.

My Uncle Forced to Change His Life

My maternal uncle **Lac, Thanh-Phong** was the chief of the general educational affairs of twenty-eight years in Phuoc-Duc School in Cholon until Saigon's last day. My aunt was a nurse in Fukien Hospital in Cholon. After she got married, they had two children (one girl and one boy), my aunt started a business. They had been in a pharmacy for many years; their pharmacy was named **Le-Quang-Hien** (Nha Thuoc Tay Le-Quang-Hien); however, their assets were controlled in 1977 because all medication came under national control. Shortly afterwards, my uncle and aunt came under the authority of the joint and co-operative society by the national government. They re-opened the Chinese herb medicine shop where sales could be made.

My uncle and his family escaped as refugees to Malaysia, and then later they re-settled in Canada in 1979. While my uncle and his family were living in Vancouver, they opened a Vietnamese restaurant named was " Vietnam Garden Restaurant ", it was near Chinatown in West Vancouver. Five years later, they visited my aunt's big family in New York. Later, they migrated to Toronto from there. My uncle who is the first formed member of the committee for his alumni association in Toronto since 1977 and in Los Angeles in 1995, held each year on December 01, as Fukien School birthday, since the school was built in 1907 in Cholon, Vietnam.

一九九七年五月十九日籌組福中校友會全體籌備委員狂歡迎會中合影

*7th from the left is my uncle **Lac, Thanh-Phong**, and 10th from the left is my aunt **Lac-Dai Van Phuong** who received a warm welcome from the whole committee of the Fukien School and their alumni association held gala in a Chinese restaurant in Toronto in 1997.*

During the Vietnam War, my uncle owned pharmacy named **Le-Quang-Hien** *in Cholon, on the left who is standing beside my uncle is his friend. My aunt is standing on the right holding a little boy, who is their son* **David Lac.** **David** *is now a dentist in New York.*

1973年校慶盛宴中難忘的歡樂情景
由左起：楊明中學訓導主任、鄧氏敬校長、馬惠芳老師、
駱青峯總教務主任。

*From left: **Duong-Minh High School's** affairs. The **Phuoc-Duc School's** principle Dang, teacher Ma, Hue-Phuong, school's affairs Lac, Thanh-Phong and Ha, Duc-Tuong was gathering together in a cheerful banquet in Cholon, Vietnam, 1973.*

福中91週年校慶頒發聘書予顧問們

91st annual celebration for the counselors who received their honor awards *from the* **Phuoc-Duc School**, an old boy, in Toronto, Canada 1998.

福中91週年全體會員和嘉賓竪立唱校歌
An alumni association and guests are standing to sing the anthem
of Phuoc-Duc School as the 91st annual celebration in Toronto, Canada 1998.

洛杉磯福校校友會歡祝88週年校慶:大家唱校歌・越海
蒼茫、閩山遠隔、眷懷祖國殷夕、一生教育幸流光、、、
88th annual celebration in Los Angeles, U.S. 1996.
[All photographs taken from the information guide of the
Phuoc-Duc School Alumni Association from Toronto and Los Angeles]

"The anthem of **Phuoc-Duc School**"

*My uncle and his family visiting us at **Mining Museum**
in Squamish, British Columbia, Canada in 2001.*

Literature, Art and Music Under Communist's Controls

Vietnam has a varied tradition from their heritage of the old regime system that included the Literature, Art and Music.

Before the fall of Saigon in 1975. <u>Literature,</u> was factual and fictional, journalistic writing, printing or advertising, and political criticism and practical writing. Also, sculptures, handicrafts, such as epic poetry, prose, novels and essays. <u>Art,</u> included a new forms of musical drama, known as *cai luong,* and spoken drama known as *kich noi,* emotional films, western operas, oratorios, lyrical drama all around the world. <u>Music</u>, such as classical, love and sadness, hit and popular songs, most from Americans, Taiwan and Hong Kong, and more the exploits of Vietnamese heroic and patriotic songs of the old regime systems, were heard everywhere in southern Vietnam.

As a result of that, the regional Vietnamese Cadres came to register a numerous part of the South Vietnamese houses, and from provinces to cities in the infancy of the revolution period. They confiscated, burned, and destroyed more than the entire old regime of South Vietnam's current dong, and culture. By and large, this included all kinds of cultural novels and educations, such as love and affectional novels, historical novels, and other popular novels, records, cassette tapes, videocassettes and movies. On the contrary, if we defied the rule, we would be sent to into so-called re-education zones to be " brainwashed " under their programs by the Communist government.

However, the Communist Party of Vietnam criticized all the above as *corruptible* and *filthy culture* and *dirty education*. Especially in the south, all literature, art, and music were to be under the government's careful and strict controls. Since they had despotic power and political control of the Vietnamese people, they snatched the people from their natural freedom of speech, thought, and human rights.

As a matter of fact, we had been trapped; dominated, and persecuted to something that burns within the conscience of every South Vietnamese person even to this day.

I was among the victims too, since I felt there was no future, fun, and joy in my life under the Communist Party. I would be ruined.

People Planning to Escape

In 1976, the Communist unified the North and South into the one nation of Vietnam. They took control of the government of the unified country and Saigon was renamed Ho-Chi-Minh City.

As a result of that, after April 30, 1975, there were many Vietnamese people from every region who tried to flee from the country. About two million adults and children, both of Vietnamese and Chinese ancestry left Vietnam as refugees. Furthermore, thousands of Chinese have been expelled from Vietnam.

*The Vietnam refugees starting escape on small wooden boats after the war. [Photograph by **Wendy Luc**]*

The Vietnamese refugees had a hard struggle just to get a new life although more than two million people have risked lives to escape from the country, but half of this number died on the high seas! Most escaped by boat while others fled overland through Cambodia and Thailand.

The small escape boats were always overcrowded, other starved on deserted isles. Many Vietnamese refugees landed temporarily on island shores, and thousands of them were victims of rape, robbery, physical beatings, and so on. They spent countless days in squalid refugee camps and were eventually forced repatriate Vietnam.

However, some refugees escaped notice but when they were caught, the Communist put them in jail to brainwash them and sent them to hard labor camps.

A small escape boat of **Long-An** *was starting out of country from Cholon about 30 kilometers after war ended in 1975.*

On the contrary, the lucky ones escape to land in Hong Kong, Malaysia, Singapore, Macau, Thailand, Philippines or Australia to live in the refugee camp they made there. More than seven hundred thousand Indochina refugees have been integrated since April 1975. And since 1980, additions of thirty thousand more Vietnamese refugees have resettled in the United States of America. Other countries, such as Great Britain, Australia, Canada, West Germany, France, Sweden and some of the neighbor countries in Europe offered their residence and citizenship.

The refugees of Vietnam (the lucky ones) had escaped successfully to the land of their escape since the war ended.

Our First Plan to Escape from Cholon

I still remember our first escape attempt.

In the summer of 1977, my nephews, nieces, and I, all seven of us tried to leave the country but all our plans went up in smoke because of the theft of our gold by dishonest people that prevented us from going.

It was a late, hot afternoon. We were starting to leave Cholon and wore plain simple clothing to avoid police or public attention. We did not carry anything in our hands when we tried to escape.

At one o'clock in the afternoon, we were started in Cholon by taking two taxis to Ben Bach Lang of Saigon. It was about twenty minutes away. From there we were going to take a ferry to Cat Lai country, which took about half an hour.

When we arrived in Cat Lai, we had to transfer to a *Lambreta*. This kind of Lambreta had seating capacity for up to ten people, and so we were altogether on this Lambreta. We went to an "out-of-the-way", place that took about twenty minutes to reach. It was an old warehouse. From there we would try to escape in the night!

First, we met a man and a lady who were about fifty years old, they were Vietnamese. They had waited to take us to the warehouse for a rest. We waited until eight in the evening. They made dinner for us. After dinner, we were walking to and fro in the back yard. We were expecting information. The man in the warehouse said that a man would come to see us at about twelve midnight, and he would take us to a boat. We were so happy to leave that night. But . . . we had waited the whole night and still the man had not yet show up. We were worried and started to doubt that he would ever show up.

Later in the night, a message came from the man saying, " Oh, no! high waves tonight! " and so we could not board a boat that night.

Then we waited until the next day for another message. Meanwhile, we did not know what to do so that we just stayed in the warehouse for the night. Then next morning, when we woke up, we got a negative message from the man, who said, " the circumstances are still bad. " Also, the man kept saying, " go home and plan it for another day. " This ran into a snag. We were immediately very disappointed. This plan had gone up in smoke.

Weeks turn into months, we missed tidings. Thus our first planned escape from Cholon ended in 1977.

74

Our Second Plan to Escape from Cantho

In the autumn of 1978, my nephew, **Ly, Tuyen-Binh**, and I tried to escape from Cholon by taking a ferry to Cantho City, which is the capital of the Mekong Delta and the region's gateway in South Vietnam. We were going in the company of my brother-in-law, and his friend's family on a boat also at night. I saw one of my chums, his name is **Huy,** and he was on same boat. Huy settled in West Germany in 1980. He visited me in Vancouver in the summer of 1983. At that time, he stated that the boat was in a terrible condition and sailed poorly. It almost sank, but finally they were on the gulf to Thailand's Refugee Camp after four days of great peril!

We had not sailed in his boat because it was very small and crowded. It seemed dangerous to step on the boat and so my brother-in-law did not feel like going on aboard. My nephew and I waited to go another day. Before we got home from Cantho City, we met two local officers, who suspected and caught us. We had stay in the regional Cantho office to report. After all we were feeling the heart sinking heavily. Then they questioned us about why we were there. They checked our luggage and they kept us there until midnight . . . we stayed there until the next morning. After obtaining a pardon, we went home because we bribed them with money.

A Tragic Escape

My niece, **Ly, Ngoc-Anh,** was twenty years old in 1978. Children begin school at a later age in Vietnam, so she was in grade eleven at the time. My mother loved her very much, and she was doing well, she was studying Vietnamese and Chinese languages. She was an excellent student.

Like numerous other young people who grew up in the South, she chose to leave rather than live under the new Communist regime. In November 1978. She made her way to Vung-Tau Beach, boarded the XXX337, a small wooden inter coastal vessel used for having cargo along the coast. She was traveling with a family who were the friends of my brother-in-law. The boat set at insight on the South China Sea. November is in the middle of the wet season, where frequent storms make for dangerous traveling on the water. Still, the journey to Hong Kong it would take three days or about one week before a refugee camp again contacted home.

It was one month later and we still had not heard any further information from my niece, which was like a stone sunken in the big sea. Our family stopped searching for proof of the sinking in 1998. No friends or relatives of people aboard have been seen since they made up the five out of every ten refugee boat, which completes their journey. This tragically perished in an attempt to escape from Vietnam.

The last picture ever taken of my niece Ly, Ngoc-Anh and me at a party at my house on March 16th, 1975, forty-three days before the fall of Saigon. The boat she was on sank in South China Sea en route to Hong Kong in 1978.

Bribing the Government

Years later, I made my successful escape.

Hour by hour, day to day, and year after year, I waited, watching for our chance to escape. In spite of the fact that it was dangerous and difficult, I was determined to leave Vietnam. It was officially forbidden to plan to escape, possibly by boat through bribery.

My brother-in-law had heard of a wooden boat only twenty-four meters long and five meters wide on which my nephew and I could get passage. Our turn had come. A close friend of my brother-in-law, Mr. **Ly, Trieu-Giang** helped us get onto the boat. Then, brother-in-law gave eleven bars of gold to Mr. Ly, who paid it to the boat's owner. He had planned the escape with us.

We knew well that the Vietnamese government was expecting people to try to escape. People escaping had to bribe provincial officers in order to be able to leave. Some refugees had escaped without paying the bribe to the Communist officials, but when they caught, they were put behind bars, and sent to concentration camps under the euphemism of *re-education camps* and sent to the infamous *hard labor camps* or exiled to hide and far away locations or condemned to life imprisonment.

Our Third Plan to Escape From Cantho

I remember on May 27, 1979, I got up extra early in the quiet morning at five o'clock. This was the morning star, the sky was black but there was little bit of dim light. I heard the cocks crowing nearby and the wild dogs barking far away, then I opened the front door, I saw just a few cars running on the streets, and a few people carrying their bamboo posts with baskets along their way.

I had my father drive me in his blue automobile *Mobilite* (a motor-like scooter), I sat at the back seat while we were riding, and we could feel the fresh air that was blowing us. It took half an hour to arrive at Cho Hoa-Binh of Cholon (Hoa-Binh market place). We were gathering there, taking a civilian bus to meet other people and my nephew, Tuyen-Binh for our evacuation. There were four buses already waiting there.

Later on, my sister, brother-in-law, and Binh met in the bus. By this time, we felt so sad that we were leaving. The buses were starting to operate at six o'clock in the morning. At this time, the sky was filled with the brightness of the sun.

We waved and said, " Good-bye! " to my father.

We would miss Saigon, Cholon, and all my friends and family!

We were on route going south from Cholon because a ferry ran between Ben-Tre and My-Tho, which was further south. Then we had a long drive from the junction of the provincial capital of Cantho. It took us six hours to reach there and we were set up in a hotel later in the day. The city of Cantho had a friendly feeling, although there was not a great deal of sightseeing to be done there. From here, the only visit was to the animated Cantho market. It is the most modern city in the Delta and is an important commercial center and river port.

Preparing to Leave Cantho
Monday, May 28, 1979

At about nine o'clock in the morning, we were in the Cantho hotel to eat breakfast. After that, two military trucks came to deliver us, thirty people in each truck. It was approximately ten o'clock in the morning when the trucks left the hotel. We were on the way and they dropped us off at a small valley where we took a rest for the rest of the day. Before we had dinner, there was a huge empty place containing about three hundred people who had stayed over night.

*This was the place we met and waited for the bus to escape for the third time at **Hoa-Binh Marketplace**.*
*[Photograph by **Ta, Khanh-Phat**]*

Tuesday, May 29, 1979

After we woke up early in the morning, everyone was still waiting for more information from the ship owners and their friends. The local officers instructed us about the time and how to get onto the boat. It was ten o'clock at night; everybody left the huge place and started to walk one followed by the other. After we had a night walk nearby, we all gathered ashore at the boat site while it rained cats and dogs. We were waiting in the rain until midnight to load on the boat. We were all wet even when we were carrying umbrellas. Everybody felt cold and tired without sleeping all night when we gathered at night, the boat's number was **HG 3438**, we all came on board and became two in distress that made sorrow less .It took half a day until seven o'clock in the morning, an officer called out our names one by one and they made a thorough search our luggage for any money or valuables before boarding the boat. Everybody was allowed to carry only small light bags and dry food because of the boat's weight limit. My nephew and I brought just a few packages of dry food and four liters of bottled water. In the meantime, my nephew and I said goodbye to my brother-in-law, sister, and friends on that sad night. Although a mix of rain and tears kicked in the scenes, I controlled the tears in my eyes because I knew if I made my feeling worry, my brother-in-law, sister, and friends would be sadder after my nephew and I had left.

Our Departure

After entering the gate check, the crew put us near the engine at the bottom of the boat, sitting crammed in with about a hundred others. Altogether, when we left, there were four hundred Vietnamese of all ages that boarded the boat. Most were Vietnamese of descent Chinese. There were exactly seventy children, two hundred young men and women, one hundred seniors, plus, I found out later, about thirty stowaways all jammed onto the three levels of the old wooden boat, we waited nine hours there. When we felt the boat starting to leave around four o'clock in the morning, the other passengers waved and said " Goodbye Saigon! Vietnam! " We were on our way. The Coast Guard convoyed our boat and another boat out of the country's jurisdiction. We crossed the difficult barrier!

The boat was drifting on the ocean while we were headed southeast of the South China Sea. During the sailing, I felt pretty homesick for my parents, brothers, and brother-in-law, sisters, and friends. I also recalled of the time since our first plan to escape that my parents told me to write letter quickly home. To this, we tried over the hump because it was our third plan to escape. I still see every detail as if it were visualized in front of my eyes.

Escape From Vietnam
While we were sailing on International waters between <u>Thailand,</u> <u>Malaysia</u> and <u>Indonesia,</u> we journeyed for miles and miles ...!!

Life on the Seas

Wednesday, May 30, 1979

At six o'clock in the morning, the sea wind was cool... we had been sailing steadily on the South China Sea for a couple of hours when we were stopped by the Coast Guard while the other boat was well ahead of us. Sea Customs boarded our boat and began to call our names from the list that they got from the captain. They left half an hour later, after the captain gave them some Vietnamese dong. Then we continued our journey following the southeast coast.

On the way, we met the other boat and we sailed by Bay-Gia inlet, its number was **HG 2575**. Its Coast Guard escort was tied up to it, and we pulled up the two boats and stopped. The Coast Guard told us that the other boat's water pump was not working and they were sending it to the port at nearby Soc-Trang. They told us we had to take one hundred eighty of the refugees from that boat, although we were already jammed like "sardine". We knew they had bribed their way onto our boat.

Thursday, May 31, 1979

We were still waiting near Bay-Gia inlet because the Coast

Guard wanted some more money from us. Our boat was on the boundless ocean the windy rough sea and the high waves beating and rocking our boat through out the whole night. It scared us. We felt like we were trapped on an oceanic houseboat. We were waiting miserably for the winds to subside, and many passengers became seasick.

Friday, June 01, 1979

Nine o'clock in the morning . . .

It was the beginning of our third day on Bay-Gia inlet, when we saw three other boats sailing near Bay-Gia inlet from Cantho. Their boat numbers were CD 00222, CD 00666, and CD 0099. Once again, the Sea Customs invited our captain and the captains of the three boats for a meeting on their boat. They said that we had to pay a tax of two thousand Vietnamese dong. After we paid this bribe, we were all allowed to leave without an escort.

Saturday, June 02, 1979

We sailed until nine o'clock in the morning.

When we got close to Khon-Dao (Khon Island, a high security prison island), we were surrounded by the Sea Customs boats. They also wanted some valuables and Vietnamese dong from us before letting us leave Vietnam. The captain came around with a bag to ask us to give some jewelry, even a small ring, and some more money. We all took what money and valuables we had left and gave it to the captain to give to them. When the bag was full enough, the captain gave it to the Custom officers and they finally let us go. I believed that, that would be the last time we would meet the Sea Customs and Coast Guard in our five days on the ocean.

Sunday, June 03, 1979

Midnight at one o'clock.

We felt the freedom of getting out of Vietnam while we crossed the difficult barrier and we felt as free as a bird! We were sailing on International Ocean. By this time, we had lost the three other boats. All of a sudden, the wind on the sea rose, the sky grew black with clouds and the water was getting rough. We lay wind-bound for a whole night; Binh and I were really worried that our boat would sink because of the extremely strong winds at dark night! When we went up to the main deck to have a look, a cold wave splashed over our heads and we heard the waves beating our boat's hull, like the sound of battle . . . Boom . . . Huum . . . Boom . . . Huum . . . we prayed for the wind and waves to calm down . . .

We had lost our way with no land or mountain insight and the engine was not working on that dramatic night on the ocean. Powerless, the boat turned around and around on the rough sea. This was an eventful night, and people on the boat held their empty plastic bottles, containers, or life jackets close in case the boat sank.

Monday, June 04, 1979

Our engine was still broken and we were still drifting helplessly on the open ocean.

At quarter after three in the afternoon, the weather was hot and dry; we saw two large U.S. ship coming toward us. They were American aircraft carriers. Two of the American naval officers came aboard our boat and helped to fix the engine in a couple of hours. They also gave us medicine, food, fruits, cookies, milk and water enough for two or three days. On the main deck, a couple of young Vietnamese refugees were fighting and grabbing fall over for each other's food and water . . . I felt it was not a dandy thing to do, which they acted so coarsely in front of the American officers.

Later, one of the naval officer asked if we wanted to be towed to the Philippines and from there to a Vietnamese refugee camp. But the captain of our boat did not want to go there as it was his intention to land in Australia!

"Oh . . . that fool! " I thought.

I was disappointed with what our captain had told him. If I had been able to speak good English, I would have arranged to go with them. Unfortunately, the aircraft carrier had already left and we lost our chance. As a result of that, we started to navigate the ocean on our own. Hoping not being in hot water, and being attacked by pirates. At that, everyone was on needles and pins with becoming what may.

Tuesday, June 05, 1979

At approximately seven thirty in the morning. The ocean water looked brilliant in the sunlight. We continued our journey for miles and miles, and sailed to the Siam Ocean, after we had fixed the engine and had been provided with enough food and water for survival by the Americans.

Binh and I were still sitting by the engine at the bottom of the boat, and other people were also sitting in their same places. All of a sudden, I heard a boat coming so I went up to the deck. It was coming toward us, and everyone was so happy and expectant that if that would be a good boat and if they might give us supplies. Therefore, we were cheering and waving for help, and the boat came toward us, and it drew closer. We were glad but frightened from the excitement.

" Look at that! " some were saying.

Oh, no! It was not a good boat; it was a Thai pirate fishing boat! The…pirate-fishing boat came into sight only minutes and caused the sky to fall as our boat drifted on "Thai ocean."

"The pirates fishing boat!" we feared of saying that.

Before I returned to my seat, I saw a long-tailed fishing boat, about eight meters long, when it drew more closer to us. The pirates tied up to our boat and four Thai pirates jumped on to our deck. They were dark with jet long hair and skin deep-set eyes, giant legs and feet that crashed on the deck as they ran about. They were huskily built men with mean, rough attitudes. This was the first time that I had seen Thai pirate fishermen, and they hustled us for a quick check of our luggage and pointed us with their razor sharp knives, hammers, axes and heavy metal bars. They walked all around, up and down our boat throughout the whole day several times to find any valuables to take from us. They ordered us to open our mouths to see if we had any gold or diamonds hidden there, and took what people were wearing: earrings, rings, necklaces, bracelets, and so on.

The Thai pirates continued checking up and down again to dig through our entire luggage and strewed our clothing and other stuff on the boat's deck as they searched for anything value through till midnight.

Wednesday, June 06, 1979

Facing difficulties in two days in a row and these misfortunes never came alone. On a sudden; the first pirate boat was scared off when they saw another big boat's lights in the distance coming toward us. It was another pirate coming over, and the first pirate boats hastened away, and the second pulled up and dropped anchor and tied up to us, we were in a box. This second boat was bigger than the first boat and it was painted with an ornate coloring, which was approximately twelve meters long.

It was early in the morning, when more Thai fisherman jumped aboard our boat and searched us for whatever money (we mainly carried U.S. dollars.), and jewelry they could find from those of us who still had some left. Yet, the pirates did not feel that was enough, as they did not get much; therefore, they searched us two more times. Consequently, they were walking back and forth searching the whole day.

Finally, when they realized there was not any more valuables to find, they became angry. I was really stunned by the Thai pirates, and my heart felt tense, while sitting crammed at the bottom of the boat.

It was unfortunate, for the pirates took four young women to their boat and raped them. A couple hours later, the pirates returned the women to our boat, and they were crying their eyes out . . . .. Their families streamed with tears, crying over their daughters' anguish. Other people on the boat were comforting those women and their families. The whole incident had a dramatic effect on all the refugees.

About five o'clock that afternoon, the pirate sentry alerted with his shipmates. Soon after we noticed a third largest boat with an ornate decoration, was a colorful feature of the Muslin South. It was about seventeen meters long. This boat was gradually coming toward us, so the second pirate boat quietly slipped away, as the third boat came into view. As the ship drew closer, I saw the headman, pacing the deck, carrying a kind of a long barreled pistol. Eight Thai pirates boarded our boat. They were especially vicious. About twenty minutes later, they were threatening us with sharp axes, knives, and hammers; they looked disheveled and mean. They immediately demanded money and valuables. By that time, we had survived two previous pirate attacks, we had nothing. They began screaming, barking demands as they paced back and forth on the deck. I really did not know which was worse, an angry pirate before he found money, or the anger they feel when they left empty-handed. Their hand gestures became more frantic as if to somehow compensate for one not understanding Thai. They directed their attention toward our kitchen on the boat. They found some thermos flasks and broke them all, they were all tossed and smashed in the galley. The first two groups had ignored our provisions, were satisfied with the money and gold we had surrendered. Desperate, these pirates slashed and ripped through some of our sacks of rice. They searched the kitchen area, which went on for fifteen minutes. The galley search yielded no gold bars or diamonds.

As night fell, they continued to search with flashlights and lanterns. Sleep was impossible. As the night wore on, we began to fear the worst. Our thoughts turned to the stories that we had heard about the pirates boarding ships empting gold and valuables. Scenes of unrelenting violence, murder, bloodshed and anger. Children were crying, and adults sat motionless and wide-eyed . . .

Thursday, June 07, 1979

At midnight, it was an intense dark night around the open ocean, but I could hear huge waves hitting the boat.

As their final deed, the pirates went below desks and begun chopping into the deck and hull wall to see if any valuables were hidden there. They were rioting throughout the whole boat in the whole night. Water was leaking through the gashes, they had hacked in the hull. We were all afraid that the pirates would sink our boat. By that time, we were worried enough that we over came our fear; however, we quickly stiff-armed them. We asked them to please not break the hull. Soon, the crew and we were carrying water out of our boat. In spite of the fact that, our entire luggage had been searched thoroughly. Each pirate wanted to check for himself. Consequently, they continued to check our luggage for hours until they were all satisfied that there was nothing to find.

Since the pirates had boarded our boat, we were all scared stiff and felt the feeling of stress in our situation.

Weakened by the duress, there were five dead that I had seen so far: four seniors and one child. The anguish of grief and sickness caused by depression and a shortage of food and water during our long trip had taken their toll on these poor souls. After they were dead, their bodies were thrown into the cold water of the Thai ocean. We prayed that would have a good life in another world.

We were jammed in the stuffy confines of the over crowded

boat squished together like sardines in a tin. We were weary of the pirates' harassment day after day, night after night. Although we had eaten in the days since the pirates had come, we were not hungry, for thirst was stronger. Most of the refugees were worried that they would die on the ocean; we did not know what was going to happen next.

The pirates took away our compass and disabled our engine and destroyed the boat's instruments, so we could not go anywhere, and they kept a careful watch to make sure we got tied up.

Later, at midday, one of the pirates with his long hair and smell of salted fish walked up to me and asked me to give him my silver necklace with a pendant that I was wearing. My heart was pounding, so I quickly gave him my silver. If I did not give it to the pirate, I was wondering whether the other shoe would drop. I was nervous and so relieved when he finally walked away . . .

It was a hot, sunny day; I guessed it was about three or four o'clock in the afternoon. I did not wear my watch as I had it in a safe place on the boat. The watch was the first one I had ever owned, and it had been given to me from my mother as a reward for good marks in high school years ago.

Out of the blue, the pirates rushed everyone onto the main deck and ordered all females to stand on one side, and males to stand on the other side. The pirates made the women take off their tops including their bras in order to clearly see if anything might be hidden there. On the male's side, the pirates searched each of our T-shirts and pockets. We could not stop the pirates nor to protect all females on our boat; it was a sad sight. Some pirates also went below decks so they could concentrate on searching our luggage while we were on the main deck and out of the way.

We were still standing there on the main deck, baking under the blazing sun and we were all so thirsty we were dripping with sweat. Some of the kids and seniors looked tired and sick; at last, they could no longer keep standing so they sat and lay down on the deck for a rest. The whole time the pirates were on our boat, they searched our stuff for the seventh time, within the three pirate boats, we felt great pressure and stress.

After six o'clock in the evening, at sunset, the ocean air temperature was falling and a cool wave splashed over our heads and the waves began beating on our boat's hull, we felt like we had just woken up from a nightmare.

Unexpected, up in the sky an airplane appeared and flew over our boat in the Thai Ocean. . . The pirates ran to their boat and sped away.

"Say grace!" we said.

In the same breath, we thought that anything else happened it might grow worse later by surprise or the worst just being over! However, we were in a mixture of grief and joy when we cheered as the plane flew overhead. We all went back to the spot where we were seated and gathered all our belongings from all around the boat decks. By that time, it was too dark on our boat to do anything, since the pirates had broken and damaged many of the lights on board. It seemed like we were living in a dark world while we lay waiting for sleep to come. We were still very shaken and fearful from the three days of abuse by the pirates; we felt disturbed in our minds until the next day.

Friday, June 08, 1979

For three days we had been robbed seven times of back-to-back searched by three different pirate-fishing boats on the Siam Sea. We had faced a difficult time and had a close brush with death, which was just a walk over!

Day turned to dawn, and we got up at sunrise in the morning

after those frightening days dominated by the rough Thai pirates, but we also had good sleep like we had not had since the trip began. In fact, everyone was feeling refreshed and relaxed without the stress that we had felt under the pirates. We were all preparing light snacks, hot drinks, cold drinks, and dried food from whatever was left in our luggage for the day and left it in a pot in the kitchen for them to help themselves. Around noon, the sky became dark and our boat crossed out of the Thai ocean into the International waters between Thailand and Malaysia. We were alone on the surging ocean; there was not a ship in sight, neither land, nor island, nor mountain.

Moment's later, lighting bolts set the clouds aglow; then thunderous claps followed. Suddenly, the sea thrashed and stormed angrily at that time. This went on for about two hours, and our boat slowly sailed through the ocean current. A few people on the boat became seasick, the children were screaming and crying. We took advantage of the rain and collected water in containers for later use, but that still was not enough. That meant we would be forced to conserve water with a maximum of care, providing just enough water to those who urgently needed it.

After it stopped raining, the sea calmed down for a while. At about three o'clock in the afternoon, the engine stopped again and our boat drifted powerless on the ocean. Once more immobile, we were all very worried that the pirates would return or that bad luck would make anything happen to us. Once again, the captain and his crew worked for hours on the engine head from evening until late night, most people felt the same, became tired and bored while we waited.

Saturday, June 09, 1979

Around one o'clock in the morning, we were facing the dark night, the wind was harsh, and the waves were rough.

Our engine was working after the captain and crew finally managed to repair it. Everybody was happy and made a good wish and we hurried on our way. We journeyed for miles and miles, from dark to dawn, and dawn to dusk until the next morning. We had made it to the border of the Malaysian ocean.

Sunday, June 10, 1979

We kept sailing on our way throughout the morning.

We were still on the open ocean and the air was very foggy; we could not see very far, but we could smell the salty water of the sea and felt the chill of the moist air. I was on the deck top to breathe a little better after hours of the stifling air below the deck. For many long days we had been sitting for endless hours pressed up against each other, and many of us were suffering from back pains, numb legs, and sore arms and necks. It was a very bad situation and the conditions below decks were getting grim.

We had been in sea for more than ten days now. A couple of seniors who had been very weak and in poor health had died by this time, and their families had wrapped them and threw the poor souls into the ocean. We all felt sorrow, and that just added to our misery.

About one o'clock that afternoon, we were still sailing and saw something far in the distance but we did not know what it was.

"It looks like land!" some were saying. Our boat was getting closer and soon we could see that it was a structure of some sort.

"Look at that!" everybody said happily pointing and getting excited.

"It is not land, it is probably a dock", we were all guessing and saying that. We grew closer and closer to it and could see it very clearly now.

"Yahoo!!" we yelled.

"It is a mining platform!" we were all really cheerful to say so.

It was the **West Shore No VII**, an oil-mining platform in the Malaysian ocean. Our captain put the anchor down into the ocean and tried to ask the Malaysian officers to permit us to land.

We respectfully waited for their answer that came approximately two hours later. They would not allow us aboard. Instead, the Malaysian officers gave us just enough food and water to provide for our immediate needs only. In the meantime, some of us rushed to write messages and reports of our progress and asked the Malaysian officers to sent them to our relatives in Vietnam. As we were going to leave the West Shore mining platform, our captain tried to start the engine, but the motor was broken again. We got Malaysian engineers from the mining platform to come over to our boat to help repair it. They did a good job and after that it was really to perform. We pulled up the anchor and turned to navigate the ocean and once again were on our way.

"Bye-Bye!" we said to the Malaysian officers and their friends as we left.

Our captain changed directions, and we sailed southeast from the Malaysian ocean. We went non-stop through the dark night, covering miles and miles.

I believe that our captain had been mixed up in his directions and he had steered us the wrong way again, and we were going still around and around on the ocean the whole night.

On the surging ocean, the waves tirelessly beat on our boat's hull while we slept in our seats. This still had not let up the next morning.

Monday, June 11, 1979

Ten o'clock in the morning. It was a hot and really sunny day.

By this time, our motor was not working at all, and we floated on the ocean again. Helplessly, we really thought that anything could happen to us. We were watching, the horizon for signs of help. Hours later, we spotted a big ship coming toward us.

"My goodness . . . It is a Russian boat," we all said.

Twenty minutes later, it was apparent that it was a large Russian cruse liner approaching us. Because of that, we were worried and frightened for we thought the Russian ship would tow us back to Vietnam . . .? We felt fidgety and thought it was hopeless as their landing craft sped towards us.

When the Russian officers came aboard, we were expecting the worst but were overjoyed. Later; however, they came aboard our boat to find out that all they wanted from us was information.

"Oh . . .. Thank God!" I whispered.

Yet, they wanted to help us. The Russian officers not only gave us food and water but also tied a rope to our boat, and towed us for four hours to the Indonesian ocean.

It was late afternoon before we reached the Indonesian inlet. The Russians untied our boat and left us floating in the ocean, as they could not enter Indonesian waters. Our engine still did not work and our boat had been letting in water from outside waves through the axe holes in its hull. The crew and us were bailing water all through the afternoon in the Indonesian inlet.

Tuesday, June 12, 1979

Eight o'clock in the evening. Later on, the wind was rising at night; we were so scared that something bad would happen to us, because no one could suggest that from our navigation the survival hung in the balance. At that time, we were still bailing water and watching out for safety.

Soon, we had the engine running again but we were lost without the headlights and the compass needle that the pirates had taken. Therefore, the captain was not willing to proceed forward as the boat might hit a rock or run a-ground on any of the countless islands in this area. So, we were waiting for the light of dawn.

Later in the dark, most of the people on the boat were tired and fell to sleep. The children were exhausted, grumpy and tired, too.

Reaching Land on Keramut
Wednesday, June 13, 1979

Just before dawn, our boat was still on Indonesian water. By this time, I stood up and walked to the boat deck, the breeze was cool and windy, and I felt refreshed for a while. Soon, it was six o'clock; I could see the ocean now, so the captain began sailing into the Indonesian inlet. At eleven o'clock on that morning, I saw some small Indonesian fishing boats that were not far away and every refugee was cheering for the success escape to the land (see page 105 picture of our boat the HG 3438). The boat people and I yelled, flashed and waved our white T-shirts and towels upon which we had inked " S.O.S ", we whistled, and shouted loudly for help, and we banged pots and pans as loud as we could.

There! It was a heartbeat away from the "Indonesian Ocean." And they spotted us to shore where we landed on the Indonesian island of **Keramut.**

Later on, we all filled out registration forms, which our captain gave to the local officer; then we entered a gigantic opening hall where we stayed temporarily for two nights. We were treated to hot meals, and safe rest for two nights and three days.

*There! Our success excape boat **HG3438, suffering and drifting** on the Pacific Ocean from May 30 to June 13, 1979, after reaching land on the **Indonesian Island of Keramut**.*

Kuku Island Refugee Camp
Friday, June 15, 1979

We left **Keramut Island** at about six o'clock in the evening, and sailed to **Kuku Island** in the Indonesian inlet. We got there at eight o'clock at night. Kuku Island was an established temporary refugee camp, which contained about fifteen thousands Vietnamese refugees later on. While our boat reached Kuku Island, the tide was low and we had to wade twenty meters across the water and the cold sea breeze to the shore. On our way, we noticed eight other boatloads of Vietnamese refugees on shore in makeshift camps. We were one of the eight to arrive. After getting out of the boat, everybody only cared about his or her selves in the camp life.

Mr. Ly, rejoined my nephew and me on the beach shortly after we landed as we walked on the sand, feeling happy to put down all our luggage. Mr. Ly sent me to find a hut and a good location and that was the first thing I did when I got to Kuku Island that night. Then I wondered off to talk to some Indonesian people and I arranged for them to build a frame for a big hut for the next day, it cost $50. U.S. By that time, it was late at night and when I got back to where Mr. Ly was, waiting on the beach, we put a plastic sheet on the sand and slept on the ground throughout the rest of the cool, dark night and we spread a couple of layers clothes on the sand to keep warm.

The next morning, the two Indonesians came to help to build a hut frame; they spent the whole day to build. Later, they showed us where to get roofing material: a long walk up the mountain to cut branches with leaf blades. While we were making the hut, we met two new friends; they were **Lam** and **Tan**, a sister and brother as a refugee from Vietnam. They were building a hut beside us and suggested that we lived together and work together to build a larger hut. Tan was good at making a frame and wall and roof covers. We saw the sense in their suggestion.

Life on Kuku Island

I lived on **Kuku Island** for about six months, during which time more than twenty boats arrived. On Kuku Island, we had a leader, his name was Hoang, he was a former South Vietnamese Army general, and his Second-In-Command, his name was Thong. He was a lawyer, who established the rules and organized our community. They told us where to set up camp all in tidy rows, where to build public washrooms along the beach, how to get on the Red Cross Food Roster, and how to fill out transfer requests, etc.

In our camp, there was an Education Center, which provided a basic English, French, and German programs for those who were interested. The instructors were volunteers from the camp and some Americans, and Europeans from the International Red Cross, and a Committee of Education. They worked together.

One of our huts in which we lived in Indonesia, **Kuku Island** *Vietnamese Refugee Camp in 1979.*
From left to right: **Johnny** *(myself),* **Hung, Nghia, Mr.Ly, Vy, Hue,** *and my nephew* **Binh.**

There was a medical hut which had doctors and nurses aids from France, Germany and U.S.A. On a daily basis they provided us all with checkups, treatments, medication and drugs.

There was a court hut on Kuku Island to uphold the island's rules where cases of wrongdoing were submitted and heart twice a week.

A helicopter-landing pad on top of the mountain allowed representatives of the International Red Cross and of The United Nations from Germany, Sweden, Holland, Norway, Switzerland, England, Australia, U.S.A. and Canada to visit our island.

During my stay, most of the refugees helped to build a huge Buddhist Temple on top of the mountain and others built a huge Catholic Chapel near the camp.

There was a market place where Vietnamese carried on retail business and traded with each other in huts on the beach side. They sold food, cooking ware, fresh vegetables and fish, which were all delivered to them from the Indonesians. Some stood nearby offering to buy and sale gold bars, rings, chains, watches and jewelry and more items, which they pulled from their pockets.

They also exchanged U.S. dollars to Indonesia rupiah. For U.S. $50. or 25,000 Indonesian rupiah, we could buy a hut. One ounce of gold bar was worth to 162,000rp and U.S. $1 was worth between 500rp and 620rp. Sending a telecommunication cost 400rp. Mailing a letter was 500rp, 700rp, 1500rp depending on the type of mail service needed. But for me, I did not spend any rupiah for the stamps. I was sending my mail when the Refugee Red Cross, or the representative of The High Commission of United Nations was visiting us. I would ask them to deliver my mail for me. I wrote about twenty letters to Vietnam while I was living six months in Kuku Island.

While I was there, I met many friends who I had known from Saigon and Cholon, an outlying district of Saigon. I also met a few of new friends from the camp including the people from our ship.

Kuku Island had been an uninhabited island before the Vietnamese had sought refuge there, because of the Vietnamese War, the world's consciousness, and the news, focused on the Vietnamese refugees.

As a result of that, The High Commission of The United Nations, The Catholic representatives, and The Refugee Red

Cross dropped off supplies to the Vietnamese refugees on Kuku Island once a week, and made great improvements to the campsite. So, no one got ill or went hungry.

I enjoyed living on Kuku Island very much, despite living in a small hut with ten people. Some huts housed from two to ten people depending on their size. Our camp was near the beach with many mountains beside it; we faced the mountains and sea, and received sun every day.

We could climb a mountain, climb on the trees or in the jungle for fun; there were many trees in the mountains. We would chop down a tree, and chop off a branch for our cooking fire. To relax in hot weather, we would walk or hike through the quiet green forest on the mountain for miles and miles where we could hear water gurgle coming down from the peaks above through the forests. We often bathed and wash clothes at the stream in the sun's rays. We boiled water from the upper stream for drinking and cooking. On the beach, we would sunbathe and swim in the warm ocean every day.

Camp life became routine. Each day I would get up at seven o'clock in the morning, have a cup of cool water, or hot "oval tine", and cook congee (rice broth) with bean curd, and other preserved vegetables for our breakfast. Sometimes, I walked up the mountain for exercise, hiking through the forest on the mountain or I would walk to the beach side for a few deep breaths of fresh sea air.

When it was my turn to bring a tree to camp for firewood, I would not leave the mountain before I had chopped one down and removed the branches and leave, so I could roll it down to our hut.

In the camp, each of us who lived together was responsible for bringing down a tree or branch once a week. They are: **My-Que** and **Van-Hung** (sister and brother), **Thieu-Hung** and **Thieu-Nghia** (brothers), and **Vy,** who are Mr. **Ly**'s friend's sons. We were all familiar with each other since we had been shipmates for the last fifteen days. Others **Vuong Lam** and **Tan**, we met at the camp on the second day after our arrival while we were building our hut. Tuyen-Binh who is my nephew, and me. The two elder males in our hut, Mr. Ly and his friend, **Bang**, did not have to go to the mountain to carry the wood.

Additionally, each of us took turns. I was not to cook or make food for them nor for myself, as I was not a good cook because I would ruin any meal I tried to prepare. I only knew how to cook rice and congee that was it! Consequently, I washed the dishes and bowls after we had finished eating.

At noon, I would help people in the camp to fill out their supply requests and application forms for their resettlements.

In addition, I often went around to talk to people and would look forward to seeing the leader and friends in the camp to get information about or announcements from The United Nations High Commission, and International Red Cross. Whenever they were later to visit us, we would worry about whether or not we would get the supplies we need. The days they did not conduct, resettlement interviews passed slowly; we all had to leave the island for our new lives in a new country.

Between three and four o'clock in the afternoon, I would swim in the ocean with our friends from the camp.

Between six and seven o'clock in the evening, we would eat supper, and clouds of gnats would swarm around to eat food from our bowls. After dark, without power in the camp, we would light candles and lanterns so we could see what we were doing.

After eating supper, I always turned on the radio to listen for the news; it was an Australian radio station broadcasting of Chinese Voice program from Melbourne City. I had written a letter requesting that they played three songs that I liked, they were "Miss You So Much", "Under The Banyan Tree", and "Do Not Go Home Today" with the letter I had asked the station to forward a message to my relatives and friends in Vietnam, saying that we were all okay, and were staying in the refugee camp on Kuku Island in Indonesia. Every night, I followed the news on the radio and listened to them play music until ten o'clock. Then I fell asleep.

There were a lot of tall coconut trees around our camp, and when it was windy and stormy in September and October, a number of dangerous accidents occurred. Some of the older coconut trees were toppled onto huts, and a few Vietnamese refugees received minor injuries. Many other huts were damaged by windstorms often losing their roofs. Sometimes the heavy rain caused the flooding of the stream. We were living in the fear through nights of rainy season in September and October storms; we slept little while listening for the crash of a tree through our roof!

Having spent half a year living in the camp, everyday I urgently wanted to leave it to go to a third country. The beaches and mountains already bored me and there was never anything new that I wanted to do.

After sometime, we heard a general announcement that we would be leaving as soon as possible. Each us lined up to be interviewed by a United Nations High Commission Representative. Representatives from each country that offered political asylum checked over applicants' back grounds, personal data including their education, job skills, former occupations, marital status and relatives.

Applying for a New Country of Residence

I had put on my application form that my principal choice was Canada since my uncle and aunt's family were living in Vancouver at the time. My second choice was Australia because I believed that it would be warm there since it is in the Southern Hemisphere. I had to wait expectantly to hear which country would quickly take me first; then I would go to live there.

While filling out applications, a friend, who was my classmate's brother, his name is **George Tran**, became my friend of having traveled over the deep blue sea. George filled out his application form with the same country so we would be together.

Finally! After I had my escape successfully, my dream was going to come true. Even though I had become bored I had had a wonderful time on Kuku Island. It was a favorite part of my life.

*A huge Buddhist Temple '**Quan Am**' on top of mountain ground of **Pulau Galang Island Refugees Camp, Indonesia**, in 1979.*

*I was standing on the stairs in front of the gate "**Quan Am**" temple at **Pulau Galang Island Refugees Camp, Indonesia**, in 1979.*

Pulau Galang Island Refugee Camp

By the end of the year, I left Kuku Island and moved to the **Pulau Galang Vietnamese Refugee's Camp Center** on **Galang Island.** Pulau Galang Vietnamese refugees Camp Center was a place where the United Nations High Commission could easily administer all the refugees. There were more than forty thousands of Vietnamese refugees there.

On December 15, 1979, a representative of The United Nations High Commission called my name. In the same breath, he told me that I was going to be leaving Kuku Island at the drop of a hat, and moving to another camp before going

Thousands of Vietnamese refugees were temporarily living in "barracks" 'of the **Pulau Galang Island Vietnamese Refugees' Camp Center** *in* **Indonesia** *before being resettled in the third country. [photo by* **Thai Khac Chuong**]

to a third country. They took me to the Galang Island Camp, the last station for refugees before being resettled in a new country. At the time, George was still in Kuku Island, but we would see each other again in Galang Island a few weeks later. Although I was in Galang Island, I very much missed all people in Kuku Island since we shared together our afflictions.

Galang Refugee Camp was five times bigger than Kuku Island, and there were many barracks of different colored roofs on the mountainsides. The painted roofs made it easy to identify our *barracks* and the way to go and to come; therefore, we would not loose the way we came in and went out. And it was easy for our leader and for the refugee representatives who walked up the mountain to visit us and to find their way around.

On Galang Island, we had our fuel, food, rice, oil, salt, water and other special needs provided by The United Nations High Commission of Refugees, The International Red Cross, and Catholic groups. I stayed there for three months and eight days.

Finally, The Representative officer of Land Immigrants called my name on the ground telling me that I had been accepted by Canada. I was so happy that I admitted quickly; a few months had passed since I had filled out the application. And I passed the health examination and my file checked out to be okay. Actually, Canada had been my first choice and my purpose had been to apply for landing status there. On the other hand, my nephew's first choice had been Sweden because he had lots of brothers and sisters there. My nephew left Kuku Island and he settled to his first choice in Sweden in a few months after I left Kuku Island.

Pulau Galang to Singapore

Monday, March 24, 1980, about twelve noon, George and I prepared all luggages and caught a small Singapore ferry going from Galang Island to the refugee camp in Singapore. Four hours later at four o'clock in the afternoon, we arrived at the Singapore seaport immigration office. Then, from there, we were bussed at quarter to five in the afternoon to a Vietnamese Refugee Camp at **Sembawang Ship Yard** on View Road in Singapore. We were there for three days and two nights. During those days and nights I was very excited by the beautiful view of the modern skyline in the "Lion City", George and I walked out of our camp to view Singapore at night specially. We took a bus down town to sightsee and shop. I exchanged my Indonesian rupiah for Singapore's dollar at the watch store, and purchased a Seiko. I also bought many Chinese cassettes and English books. We had a bowl of wonton noodle soup in a restaurant mmm . . . it tasted so good, because we had not had it for ten months and we were eager for it!

Tuesday, March 25, 1980. At three o'clock in the afternoon, it was really hot in the Lion City.

While I was walking out of our camp to find a telephone booth nearby, I phoned my uncle **Ta, Thanh-Han** but he was not home as he was in his office, and my aunt, **Giang-Hoa,** received my call. I had a pleasant conversation with my aunt. Before I tried going to their house, my uncle and his driver Mr. Shiao came into our refugee camp from work in the bank at five o'clock in the afternoon. I was so excited that it warmed the cockles of my heart to see my uncle right there! Half an hour later, George went with me, we were all seated in uncle's car with Mr. Shiao, we had a good visit at my uncle's house and I met my cousin **Kien-Minh** at home as well. I had not seen them for four years since they landed in Singapore. They still live in a skyscraper on twenty-third floor of the Pearl's Center in downtown.

Then we shopped and walked around the town, my aunt bought me some English books, and my uncle gave me a portable stereo radio cassette. After that, they invited us to a famous restaurant for a super supper meal. After the meal, we planned a farewell meeting for the next day.

Sorrowfully, my uncle passed away in 1998, at the age of seventy-six, I pray and wish him happiness in another world.

Singapore to Canada

Wednesday, March 26, 1980, at quarter after seven in the morning. It was a day with fresh air and gentle wind, I felt quite refresh on that day.

After preparing for our breakfast from a hostel in Singapore's Refugee Camp, there were about thirty of us left in the camp, and then a couple of vans came to take us to Singapore's airport. We were in a C.P Air Douglass, model CD-8. We flew for six hours and twenty minutes to Tokyo.

From Tokyo, at two fifty in the afternoon, we flew to one of Japan's military airports, and waited for one and a half hours before we left Japan to Canada. We arrived in Edmonton, Alberta Airport for eight hours and twenty minutes; later it was twelve forty in the morning. When I walked outside for the first time, there was a good and cold breeze and snow that felt as cold as a freezer. We were in the Edmonton Vietnamese Community Services hall; everybody filled out arrival forms and had our luggage checked by Canadian Customs officers. Immediately after that, we had a health examination conducted by the Health Department in the Edmonton Airport. We waited for a few hours for them to process our documents, and then we boarded a bus and were shuttled to a hotel where they had rooms reserved just for us..

...There, we ate a buffet lunch and were shown to our rooms where we were to live until more permanent arrangements could be finalized.

Our host, the Canadian government was paying the bill for our stay in the hostel, which included breakfast, lunch and dinner. They also gave us bankbooks for accounts they had set up for us with the Canadian Bank of Nova Scotia with ten dollars already in them.

My First Day in Edmonton, Canada

During my first day in the Edmonton hotel, I experienced the satisfactory feeling of my escape. When I turned on the shower for a bath, I was happy to see that the water was not yellow and polluted as it had been back in Vietnam; it was the greatest experience I had ever enjoyed! I pleasured and luxuriated in the comfort of the warm, clean pure water and private stall, and knew that my new life in Canada would be like paradise! I never forget when drinking water, think about how it was made.

George and I stayed in the hostel for six days while we waited for our immigration papers to arrive. By then we already had heard from our sponsor, John, in Vancouver, British Columbia, and had arranged for us to go there. We got to Vancouver, British Columbia, on Monday, March 31, 1980.

Arrival in Vancouver

Monday, March 31, 1980, about two o'clock in the afternoon (in Edmonton time).

George and I left Edmonton Airport; we flew in a 737 Boeing airplane directly to Vancouver Airport, British Columbia. **The Franklin Baptist Church** in Vancouver sponsored us to come to Canada.

Our plane was late, when we arrived at Vancouver Airport at three o'clock in the afternoon. The church members were already waiting for us at the arrival gate. There were the elders **Mr. John Olax Anderson, Mr. Sam Lau,** and **Pastor, Edwin Kong.** They helped us settle in new rooms at the resident house in East Vancouver that Monday afternoon.

At about six thirty in the evening, our church members treated George and me to dinner at a Chinese cuisine restaurant on Victoria Drive in Vancouver where we lived nearby. After we had finished the good dinner, they took us home and we had a good rest throughout the night.

Certainly, my first day in Vancouver was a good and peaceful, silent night and I had never had such a great rest in my life as I was in a state of bliss to the contrary since I was living under the Vietnam flags, during the Vietnam War, I was forced to endure ordeals.

In spite of the peace and quiet, I felt homesick at all times, because of the fact that all my relatives and old friends were in Vietnam. In particular, the first few months after my arrival in Canada, I had bad dreams about being in the war in Vietnam, trying to flee from the Communist onslaught, and I becoming a refugee in my attempt to escape by any means.

Mr. John Anderson always gave a ride to the Franklin Baptist Church each Sunday morning. We met many new friends there; they were friendly, helpful and enjoyed us. Also, they were praying for us. I really appreciated their warm hands and warm welcome.

Life in Vancouver

Between the years 1975 and 1985, the last decade, which thousands more Vietnamese perished from Vietnam to their third country. At that time, having the arrangement for the Vietnamese refugees to come to Canada at the service centers and settlements individually all over the country, such as Vancouver where I am living now. This was caused and sponsored by the Canadian society concerns to whom to thousands Vietnamese refugees left from the refugee camps from places such as Hong Kong, Singapore, Malaysia, Indonesia, Thailand, Philippine and many more. In Vancouver, British Columbia, we have seen many free Vietnam refugees attend the Solidarity Conference in their community. The Conferences are held each year on April thirtieth at community centers and halls. However, each year in Vietnam, the government celebrates the thirtieth of April as their regime's Victory Day. No doubt, today the refugees and their younger generations from Vietnam can be found in Asia, Australia, Canada, Europe and various parts of the U.S. protesting this occasion.

Living in Vancouver, I certainly enjoy people with their gentle and peaceful attitudes along with their sense of humor. It has brought me an unforgettable new life. I intend to stay in Canada forever. My family and I love it so very much.

Oh, Canada, we love you!

In principle, now at least all of free Vietnamese, including myself, have their human rights returned, including freedom from fear, freedom of action to develop their own lives, as they desire. As an oversea Vietnamese, I have learned a lot about the American ways. I no longer am a Vietnamese refugee but a Canadian citizen. This fulfills one hundred percent of my expectations after having escaped, tolerated and suffered in Vietnam under the Communist forces.

*In the year 2000, one of the Community Centers on Fraser Street in Vancouver, British Columbia, Canada, holds a **Solidarity Conference Day** for the Free Vietnamese Refugees each year **on April 30th**. The flag shown above at the front entrance was **the Republic of Vietnam Flag**.*
*[Photo by **Johnny Lac**]*

On April 30th, 2000. **The twenty-fifth anniversary of Vietnamese Refugees' Exodus For Freedom**, is held in Vancouver. British Columbia, Canada

[Photo by **Johnny Lac**]

*This picture was taken at Britannia School's Gym in Vancouver, B.C. Canada
on April 30th, 2002, and the Free Vietnamese Refugees are
remembering their **Day of loss on April 30th, 1975**.
[Photo by **Johnny Lac**]*

I was taking part of the ceremony at Britannia School's Gym in Vancouver, British Columbia, Canada on <u>April 30th</u>, 2002.
*[Photo by **Wendy Lei**]*

My sponsor, **John Olax Anderson** *standing beside me at a party at* **The Franklin Baptish Church** *in Vancouver, 1980.*

Picture taken at **Canada Place** *on* **Canada Day** *in Vancouver.*
[Photo by **Wendy Lei***]*

*Vancouver is the place where I am Living now while I enjoy life in the slow lanes (on the left is my son **Brian**).*
*[Photo by **Wendy Lei**]*

*While visting at the **Vancouver Public Library Central Branch**
in downtown Vancouver, British Columbia, Canada.*
*[Photo by **Johnny Lac**]*

*The culture of the **totem pole** is good for Canada.*
*[Photo by **Johnny Lac**]*

A warm visit from my parents in our living room.

All together in my youngest brother's house on my father's birthday in Vancouver, B.C. Canada, 2001.

Vietnam Today and in the Future

Today, we are looking back in a part of history of Vietnam. After the French troops left Hanoi, the Vietminh formally assumed control over North Vietnam, imposed on the country with a harsh Communist regime. Then, the U.S.A. provided assistance directly to South Vietnam from 1954 to 1975. For twenty-one years after the U.S.A. stepped in the Vietnam War as embargo was also imposed on North Vietnam during that time.

Again, today the U.S.A. trade showed and granted products and services to Vietnam in Hanoi on April 21, 1994 of which established diplomatic relations and linked namely as "Vietnamerican" in Expo' 94. It was nineteen years after President Bill Clinton emblematic the trade embargo after the fall of Saigon. Still, Clinton has visited Vietnam, Hanoi and Saigon in November 2001 for the American Marine Expeditionary Force. They will move equipments and stores for the next few years, after two decades of struggle for freedom under the Communist's totalitarian rule. Although Vietnam is an extremely poor country with a large population, it is developing economically with a more free market than in the past. By the early 1990s, known here as "doi moi", meant change to the new, or reform through the needs, this major reform to the businesses of new marketplaces and conditions, promises unprecedented prosperity. On account of *doi moi*, the Vietnamese government opened a trade with many countries to invest businesses and good performances, economic developments, and therefore the recent economic liberalized, businessmen and capitalist have made a comeback.

It is great! The fact that the people of Vietnam now have the promise of rights for the politics' protests, to give freedom of their personal worships and social services. Indeed, today Vietnam is not like an old Communist nation, but it resembles more of a socialized nation. Today in Vietnam, thousands of Vietnamese refugees can return home to visit people around the world who can conduct a business from their good opportunity to enter the Great South Saigon or the Great North Hanoi. The foreign investors in Vietnam are from America, Australia, China, France, Malaysia, Hong Kong, Japan, Singapore, South Korea, Soviet Union, Sweden, Thailand, Taiwan and United Kingdom and so on. Their project of all kinds such as: Agriculture and fishing, chemical production, food industry, wood products, oil and fuels, tourist services, hotels, buildings transportations and, etc.

The word "business", is very important to understand because you need to know how to place your money and make investments to Vietnam. Despite the fact, if you intend to become a great businessman for activity markets there, in the first place you have to be aware for the details about Vietnamese politics, cultures, societies, local manners and customs including locations: and the contrast between both the North capital in Hanoi and the South Central commerce in Saigon. Even though we know Vietnam is a unified nation now, the South Vietnamese are always expressing their feelings and attitudes, while the North Vietnamese are seldom to show what they think about their dismal personal life. Despite political reunification in 1975, some of the Vietnamese people are still not changing from their bribes, tricks, schemes corruptions, and crimes.

Although the seizure of Langson and Bangioc Fall in Vietnam belonged to China, the Chinese wanted to keep the two country's border opened wide for co-operations in the technical and travel developments. The Vietnamese Communist Foreign Minister, Le Cong Phung, has inquired this on January 28, 2002 by the VASC Orient.

Today in Vietnam, from North, the great Hanoi, to South, the great Ho Chi Minh, there are many on an outing to walk at in the night market and enjoy many entertainments like disco dancing in the halls, movie theaters, café videos and singing a hit at karaoke lounges after their hard day of work.

As yet, let's put it in black and white, although the North Vietnamese so-called it an aggressive war and abusive human rights. People went through the mill while living under their force, not for love or money, but for great pride which the Vietnamese people had defeated for many directions from their rivals and were occupying all of the land, however through it all, and now in one whole nation of modern and independent Vietnam. This point of features and to have peace and to find a state here from now on. We wished for the Socialist Republic of Vietnam to be able to open more wide trades and establish better friendship with other countries in the world's interest and connecting with its peace. I believe that the overseas Vietnamese would not have any harbor resentment in their bosom! They would also be proud of having a new and better Vietnam in this wonderful world!

Besides, when the Vietnamese citizens get an excellent tradition created by a great lifestyle in the country. Despite the fact that Vietnam is rich in many natural and potential resources, such as timber, oil, resin, medical plants, dense forests, Asiatic animals, a variety kind of birds, fishes, reptiles, and insert life proliferated. Vietnam is the third largest rice exporters from our agriculture and other products are very particular. (See page 3 for more information.)

Vietnamese food is fun to make, and delicious as French food are especially found in Vietnamese recipes. There are also wide varieties of recipes in Vietnamese food that use other international country's recipes that are elaborate meals.

Vietnam has a wonderful coastal resort, which is called Ha long Bay or "Vinh Ha Long"; it means Bay of the Descending Dragon. (See page 13). It is an area of spectacular scenes, and its limestone formations, caves, and grottos, which found North of Hai-Phong; therefore, in 1994, this amazing predominance Ha Long Bay was selected as Vietnam's second United Nations Educational Scientific and Cultural Organization (U.N.E.S.C.O).

Ha-Long-Bay

In the era of the historic Vietnam, even their life styles have not changed; yet, we wish the internal freedom to foster democracy with its respect for the rights of all Vietnamese. This freedom for the Vietnamese should be forever and ever in this wonderful world!

Today, tomorrow, and in the future, I will always miss my childhood home in Cholon and Saigon. I will also especially miss Vung-Tau Beach, a place of popular resort in my favorite beachside and facilities retreating, and the best resort over there! For the future, as I entertain a hope and desire to see the people of Vietnam have a chance to build their future from two or three decades of war.

Today in Saigon, *"Ben Thanh Market Place"*
[Photograph by **Ly, Thuong Lam***]*

Today more hotels are around in Saigon from the foreign investors.
[Photograph by **Ta, Khanh Phat**]

Many Motor-like scooters are parked together squished side by side in Saigon and Cholon. *[Photograph by **Ta, Khank Phat**]*

Today in Cholon people are rushing here and there.
*[Photograph by **Ta, Khanh Phat**]*

*My alma mater **Phuoc-Duc School** (now Tran-Boi-Co School) in Cholon of District 5.*

Thanks to All

In conclusion, I will always be grateful to be one of the fifty percent who survived their escape from Vietnam to find freedom in a democratic country.

I would also like to thank **The United Nations High Commissioner** for refugees, **The Catholic group, The Red Cross,** and *the special world conscience people and the news media* that helped to tell the world about the victims of the war. I would also like to thank *the humanity of the Canadian people!*

A special thanks to **Mr. John Olax Anderson,** an elder at the *Franklin Baptist Chapel* in Vancouver, British Columbia, Canada. John was my sponsor for coming to Canada and helping me to adjust my life in the Canadian societ. Sadly, John passed away in 1998 at the age of eighty, in the Three Link Care House in Vancouver, British Columbia, Canada. I wish him happiness in another world. Besides John, the congregation of the Franklin chapel became my second family and I bless them all.

I would also like to thank **Mr. Nhan, Kim-Tan** and **Mrs. Luu, Thi-Hoa,** my surrogate uncle and aunt from my late teens until today, they deserve thanks for saving me from the war. Sorrowfully, love you! My surrogate uncle Nhan passed away in Texas Hospital on March 22nd, 2001 at the age of seventy-five. His wife continues to reside in Houston.

I am also proud to say *thanks to both my stern father and affectionate mother for their care. My sister and brother-in-law for their ongoing support and for saving me from the war. A special thanks to my nephew* **Ly, Tuyen-Binh,** *and the people from our shipmates escaped out of the jaws of death and shared weal and woe for fifteen days during this long journey. Also thanks to all Vietnamese refugees in the camps of Kuku Island and Pulau Galang Island that shared together affliction, and agreed to work upon shares on the camps.*

Finally, a great thanks to the workplace-tutoring program sponsored by the **Hospital Employees Union** (H.E.U.) the kind volunteer tutors in the program steadfastly encouraged me to keep writing and to tell my story. Besides, I would also like to thank everyone I knew before or after my escape. Here, *I bless you for your kindness!*

From **Johnny Lac.** May / 2003, Vancouver, B. C. Canada.

Peace

(Written to all people in the world)

Peace no war!
Peace no war!

My heart contains blood.
My heart holds *peace*.
My heart will not ever hold war.

For once, I am told to end war.
Once and for all
We should have *peace*
For we have *no war.*

Please,
Peace!

By: **Jay Lac.** February, Y2K
Vancouver, British Columbia, Canada.

和平

— 寫給世界各國的同胞們 —

加拿大 駱俊遠

和平，無戰爭！
和平，無戰亂！

我的心擁有血液。
我的心熱愛和平。
我的心永遠不會有戰爭。

至少一次，我欲說停止戰爭。
堅決地
我們願意有和平
渴望世界沒有戰爭。

願意，
和平！

（寫於溫哥華，二月千禧年）

The Gift
(Written to all parents in the world)

The most precious gift,
I am told;
Is all the love
The heart can hold.

I give it to you,
You give it to me,
There's enough for the world
And the gift is free.

Will you take my love?
More precious than gold
Is the finest gift
That the heart can hold.

By: **Jay Lac.** Happy Valentine's Day-2000
Vancouver, British Columbia. Canada

禮 物
－獻給全球的父母親們－

加拿大 駱俊遠

最珍貴的禮物,
我曾說過;
它屬於一切的愛
擁有這份心意。

我贈予您的禮物,
您亦給予我,
這份心意能夠覆蓋了世界
而,無價之寶的禮物。

我的愛您能否接納?
這份禮物比黃金更珍貴
亦是最佳的禮物
它－就是我的愛。

(寫於溫哥華,聖苑倫泰節,千禧年)

Children

(Presented to all children in the world)

Children are all over the world!
Children are of all ages.
Children would need *love*,
Children would need *care*.

Children like to have freedom,
Yet;
Some are:
Fortunate, or
Unlucky . . .

Children are important people
For the future,
Like a pillar of the society
And the state.

Children are all around the world!
Lives without sorrow
And
Lives with joy.

Children are all over the world!
Wish we all had freedom and felicity,
And endless love . . .

By: **Kay Lac.** March, Y2K
Vancouver, British Columbia. Canada

孩 童
―致給全球的每一位孩童們―

加拿大 駱韋因

遍佈世界的孩童！
所有黃金時代的孩童呀。
我們願有愛護，
願有關懷。

孩童有自由欲，
但；
有些是：
幸福的，抑是
不幸的……

孩童是未來的主人翁
在將來，
是社會
是國家的棟樑。

遍佈全球的孩童們！
我們的生命裡沒有悲傷
迄今；
孩童的生命充滿歡樂。

遍佈全球的孩童們呵！
願我們永遠自由，幸福，
和無盡的愛……。

（寫於溫哥華，三月，千禧年）

Our Past

(Written to Vietnamese refugees who escaped from the motherland)

Viet-Nam, Viet-Nam!
I miss my homeland!
So much anxiety thought about thou,
Escaping for freedom, and
Leaving for future career.
Tho, tho' wearied in the journey;
A great ambition for good.

I miss my native place __ **Viet-Nam!**
An uprising in 75,
Upward in two decades;
Hurrying off yet non-stop.
Days that belong to our past,
Com what may whether it would be windy or rainy.

By
Johnny Lac
October 2001. Canada.

我們走過的日子

駱鍾福

—寫給每一位曾經逃離越南的難民朋友們—

越南、越南！
我遺失了的越南！
對您的思念很切。
為了自由而遠走他方，
為了前程而離棄故鄉。
儘管在奔波；
志在所向。

我遺失了的故鄉—越南！
七五政變，
逾廿餘年；
奔跑不休。
你我走過的日子裡，
風雨不變。

（二零零一年十月　加拿大）

Synopsis

This was the long war that my life has walked in along journey and people's lives in which is under the Vietnam regimes, in the Vietnam War, the Terror War, and the forces by the Communist government. Even today, this very moment, it is unforgettably tragic to remember **April 30, 1975** the day of Saigon's fall, and when the War was over. Vietcong cadres were outlawed. A violated peace engulfed the center of South Vietnam. Both the North and South Vietnamese people had poured out their blood and their treasure to fight in the war. The people in the south were compelled to come together to fight what always appeared to be overwhelming numbers from the north.

In the aftermath, an internal war out of the view of television cameras begins in the South. Once known as soldiers, civil servants, intellectuals, artisans and business merchants, the communist socialist government redoubled them capitalists and bourgeoisie. Property is seized. Businesses are destroyed, confiscated or nationalized. A torrent of ideological euphemisms sweeps over the country. Re-education camps are established for the powerful or the skilled. Thousands more are forcibly marched into so-called new economic zones in the jungle. Against the ideological tide pulling people landward, a steady stream flows seaward. Through a black market of go-betweens, smugglers, gold, diamonds, and dank cargo holds, the stream flows.

From 1975 to 1985, thousands set out to sea in leaking boats. Waiting off shore, pirates swarm unsuspecting boats. Murder and rape join robbery as the standard ritual. Whenever pirate's leave, the others come. Thousands more perish. Awaiting those who survived the sea journey were the refugee camps. They have to wait many years before they can be resettled in the west.

However, in the era of historic Vietnam today and the future, there are big changes the lives and better life for a modern living because of *doi moi* plans for improving things under the Socialist Republic of Vietnam!

在越南的旗幟下

UNDER THE VIETNAM FLAGS

滄海桑田路難行
堅山固川不是雲

癸未年 駱鐘福留題

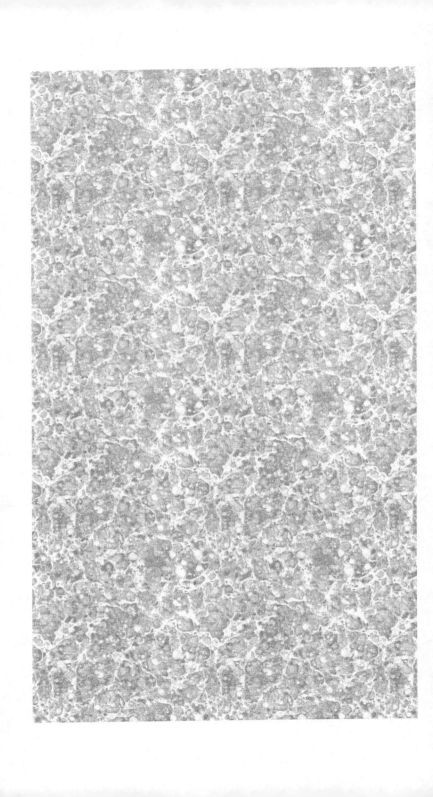

UNDER THE VIETNAM FLAGS

A long war of the history of Vietnam since the ancient have waged battle against their invaders from across the sea when the fighting grew larger and at various times it became the Vietnam War, Vietnam Civil War, the Terror War, and the terrorists were stirred by the Vietcong for what they used brutal mischief and wanton destruction to the South Vietnames until the Americans were engaged in the futile war which ended in 1975. Even today, this very moment it is unforgettably tragic to remember April 30, 197 when we said goodbye to Saigon for fear of reprisal and forces by the Communist's Regime. Thus thousands more perished during the sea journe but, only half survived to the refugee camps. In th same way, my own boat drifted on the South Chin Sea suffering from dangerous storms, dehydration and the pirates' robberies for fifteen days.

Nevertheless, from our past and in the new era of history Vietnam today and in the future, there are big changes and the lives are better for a modern living because of " doi moi " plans for the new reforms and improments under the Socialist Republic of Vietnam.

Ha-Long Bay was selected as Vietnam's second United Nations Educational Scientific and Cultural Organization